BECAUSE I'M SMALL NOW AND YOU LOVE ME

THE WORLD ACCORDING TO MY FOUR-YEAR-OLD

GINA LONDON

ALSO BY SAKURA PUBLISHING

WHEN HEAVEN CALLS

LOST EVIDENTS

DID I REALLY DO MY HAIR FOR THIS? THE DATING
DISASTERS OF A NOT SO DESPERATE GIRL

DEFEAT WHEAT: YOUR GUIDE TO ELIMINATING
GLUTEN AND LOSING WEIGHT

DEATH OF A BLACK STAR

ELVOLUTION

THE VALLEY OF ANCHOR

JOONIE AND THE GREAT HARBINGER STAMPEDE

BECAUSE I'M SMALL NOW
AND YOU LOVE ME

♦   ♦   ♦   ♦   ♦   ♦   ♦   ♦   ♦   ♦   ♦

THE WORLD ACCORDING TO MY FOUR-YEAR-OLD

GINA LONDON

SAKURA PUBLISHING
Hermitage, Pennsylvania
USA

Because I'm Small Now and You Love Me
The World According to My Four-Year-Old

Copyright © 2013 by Gina London

Sakura Publishing
PO BOX 1681
Hermitage, PA 16148
www.sakura-publishing.com

Ordering Information:
Quantity sales. Special discounts are available on quantity purchases by corporations, associations, and others. For details, contact the publisher at the address above.

Orders by U.S. trade bookstores and wholesalers. Please contact Sakura Publishing: Tel: (330) 360-5131; or visit www.sakura-publishing.com.

Book Cover and Design by Mary Raudenbush
Book Interior Editing and Design by Sarah Engdahl
Cover Photographs by Cesare Baccheschi
Interior Photographs by Gina London
Chapter Ten Photo by Irene Cascini
Chapter Eighteen Photo by Kelly Goin
Photo on Page 146 by Cesare Baccheschi

www.sakura-publishing.com

First Edition
Printed in the United States of America
ISBN-10: 0984678565
ISBN-13: 978-0-9846785-6-3
14 13 12 11 10 / 10 9 8 7 6 5 4 3 2 1

To Scotty and Lulu, of course.

ACKNOWLEDGMENTS

With heartfelt acknowledgment to everyone at Sakura Publishing and to my professional editors Derek Vasconi and Sarah Engdahl; to my equally professional, but unpaid, editors Malia Mitchell Schaefer, Cara McDonald and Scotty Walsh; to my Facebook friends who encouraged me to compile Lulu's quotes; to my Italian friends, especially Michela Lorenzini for driving us to innumerable swimming lessons and Francesca Cappelletti, without whom I never would've seen the *Giostra* ; to Mauro and Silvia Tanci, Pavlína Hábová Checcacci, Charlotte Duclaux, Chay Johnson, Heather Dahlstrom and Paola Dejuliis; to the fantastic owners and staff at Caffé dei Costanti for letting me rent a writing space for free; to Lulu's wonderful *maestre* and cooks at her preschool *Maria Bianca Bianchini;* to Jerry and Sheila Fasbender, Andrea Checroun, Brad London and Jayson Fasbender for family love; and to my ever-supportive and adventure-loving husband Scotty Walsh and our dear little daughter Isabella, aka Lulu.

CONTENTS

CONTENTS

CONTENTS

INTRODUCTION

STORIES FROM THAT
TIME IN HER LIFE
❖   ❖   ❖   ❖   ❖   ❖   ❖   ❖   ❖   ❖   ❖   ❖

AFTER ALMOST TWO DECADES in television news, I had written thousands of stories.

Some were scandalous, like President Clinton's affair with Monica Lewinsky and his subsequent impeachment. Some were funny, like my CNN "expose" revealing that all of Santa's reindeer are actually female (according to the zoological fact that male reindeer shed their antlers during the winter). Some were poignant, like the tale of the oldest living Olympic medal winner, a ninety-year-old figure skater who, although no longer strong enough to jump an axel, could still gracefully glide on the ice. And some were simply tragic, like my coverage of the aftermath of the 9/11 terrorist attacks.

I've covered everything from politics to plane crashes, crime scenes to hurricanes. No matter what the story, they all had one thing in common: they were *other* people's stories.

After my career with CNN ended, my husband, variety entertainer Scotty Walsh, and I moved to Paris with our nine-month-old daughter Lulu. Scotty had been accepted into a graduate program at the American University there, and I dove full-time into taking care of an infant while trying to navigate a new country and a new language. Life became a Parisian blur of mishaps and silly moments.

Like the afternoon I had lunch with a girlfriend at *Les Deux Magots*. Set in the posh Saint-Germain-des-Prés neighborhood, this famous restaurant had once been a favorite of Hemingway's and Picasso's. We dined *al fresco* while Lulu charmed the waiter and everyone else around us as she teethed on a piece of baguette. I felt as if I were an extra in a fantastic movie.

Then my daughter began to cry and I was jolted into reality realizing that she needed her diaper changed. I next discovered that while Parisians quite adore children, they have apparently never heard of a changing table. In the two years we lived there, I never did find one, except in Disneyland Paris, which doesn't really count.

Back at the restaurant, I had to wind my way down the narrow stairs to the cramped basement bathroom – clasping the railing with one hand and holding Lulu with the other arm as she clutched and wailed like a wounded koala. I knelt down and laid the screaming Lulu on her diaper pad right smack on the floor among the jostling high heels of about twenty women, all jockeying for one of the three tiny stall doors to open.

Whether any of them were glaring down at me or not, I'll never know. I didn't look up to see. I no longer felt like the glamorous movie extra. I was a scullery maid kneeling before a bevy of duchesses.

Now, we have moved to Arezzo, Italy. It's a medieval walled city in the center of Tuscany and the place where the heartwarming scenes from the Oscar winning movie *Life Is Beautiful* were filmed. Scotty is studying and performing *Commedia dell'Arte* in a two-year MFA program in physical theatre, and Lulu, who finally managed to grow up and out of diapers, has turned four.

She is no longer a passive participant in her overseas adventures. Now a babbling preschooler, she keeps an almost running commentary about everything she experiences. Her observations are frequently funny, often beguiling and sometimes innocently impolite.

When we moved here last summer, our Italian neighbors generously brought over some fresh red and green bell peppers from their carefully tended garden. Lulu peered down into the wicker basket as they explained that the brightly-hued veggies were called *peperoni*. The only time Lulu had heard this word was when it referred to those spicy round meat slices on a pizza back in the U.S. She looked straight up at our kind new friends and loudly announced, "Those not pepperoni 'cause pepperoni is yummy and those look icky."

Fortunately, our neighbors did not speak English.

And since that time, while they still don't know any of our language, Lulu has become fluent in theirs. She understands that *peperoni* means "peppers" (although she still thinks they're "icky") and now asks for pizza with *salami,* not "pepperoni." In fact, Lulu has learned *la bella lingua* much faster than I have. And she knows it.

"I speak Italian better than you!" she proclaims every chance she gets.

It was right about then that I realized another person's story was unfolding before my eyes - and *ears.* A person closer to me than anyone I had written about before.

My daughter Lulu is in that time of her life. That time when every child starts to realize he or she is an individual. That time of observing, learning, and pushing boundaries (and buttons).

These, then, are the quotes, anecdotes, and true stories of my daughter during that all too fleeting time in life when the world is new.

For Lulu, this time is set first in the City of Light and now here in the beautiful countryside of Tuscany.

With love and admiration for all parents everywhere,
Gina

ONE

TO BE OR NOT TO BE — BIG

• • • • • • • • • • • • •

I DREW A PICTURE OF ME TODAY SO WHEN I
GROW UP YOU WILL REMEMBER ME

FOR MOST CHILDREN, EVERYTHING is measured in either one of two time frames: "Now that I'm little" or "When I grow up." For Lulu, this is a real love-hate relationship.

On one hand, she is fascinated by the idea of getting bigger and being allowed to do more things. For instance, one afternoon she teetered over to me in my black sling-back stilettos and said, "I'm glad my legs are getting longer. I am almost ready for tall heels."

"Not quite, Monkey," I answered, "now, put those back in my closet, please."

"Can I please wear them around the house for just a little bit?"

"No, sweetie, I don't want you to accidentally fall and get hurt," I said.

"Well, can I have them when I am bigger and you are dead?"

While I am in no hurry to rush along to that particular scenario, I will say I am super-*duper* glad that enough time has gone by that Lulu has grown past the baby stage. I have heard that some parents actually adore their babies. Those little infant bundles lying there all cooing and smiling and looking like miniature, bald old men. Not me.

There just didn't seem to be that much to get excited about. From the day she was first born in Denver, Colorado, Lulu didn't coo and smile all that much. Her infantile crying jags—which seemed to stretch for hours until we finally packed her into her car seat, went for a drive, and waited for the gentle vibrations to lull her to sleep—were maddening. Her constant howling prompted Scotty to dub her the "were-*chipmunk*," since she wasn't yet big enough to earn the "were*wolf*" moniker. And speaking of sleep (or the lack thereof), even compared to my old CNN reporting days during which I regularly had to get up at 3:00 a.m. for a full day of back-to-back live shots, I never felt as perpetually nauseous as I did during those first several sleepless months in which Lulu woke up every two hours like clockwork. She didn't sleep fully through the night until sometime after a year. I don't remember precisely when. I think I've blocked it from my memory.

And diapers? I never met a diaper I liked, even if they had pictures of Snow White or Nemo on them. In fact, I had never changed a single one before our blessed arrival. She was such a little thing, yet sometimes there didn't seem to be enough wet wipes in the world. Eventually, of course, I had grown so accustomed to the process, that by the time we moved to France, I had no problem plopping her down on her changing pad right on the sidewalk of Rue de Rivoli (near the Louvre), since you can't find a changing table in all of Paris.

Before Lulu was born, nursing seemed like a wonderfully womanly and bonding experience. I looked forward to it. But when we were still in the hospital and the nurses were surrounding me, casually pulling and pinching me like I as a milking cow back on the farms in Indiana, I began to have serious second thoughts. The first day back home from the hospital with Scotty gone for the day teaching at a theater conference, I was a jangle of nerves. Lulu wouldn't nurse and, desperately afraid that she would certainly starve before the day was through, I dialed some random local number for the breast-feeding support group, La Leche League, to hear some kind reassurance from a woman who must've thought I was having a nervous breakdown. In retrospect, she was probably not all that startled by my call. I have since talked to plenty of first-time moms who have had their share of misgivings in the nursing category. It's not always easy. Thankfully, Lulu did finally get the hang of it and nursed like a cute little kitten.

Okay, so looking back, I can say that nursing, once Lulu and I finally hit a rhythm, became an extremely amazing experience. But this feeding-herself-thing that she has now accomplished? Even more amazing.

Now that she is becoming independent, our relationship has evolved into a lovely give-and-take accord, as opposed to the previous version in which I was the only one *giving* and she was just *taking* (and *taking* and *taking*). I feel like the ages of three and now four are truly magical. Lulu is a real, honest-to-goodness, human-being-individual with a growing ability to express herself. In art, she doesn't just scribble aimlessly anymore. Now she creates. Drawings of Scotty have almost realistic-looking dark hair and blue eyes, and even a body now, not just lines coming down from his head. My most recent Mother's Day card from Lulu depicted me colorfully decked out in *"tanti gioielli,"* or a lot of jewelry. I don't normally wear a lot of jewelry, actually, but since Lulu is fascinated with all the baubles I do own, she apparently wanted me to wear them all in her drawing. Along with my high heels, she also regularly asks if she may have all my earrings and necklaces "after you're dead."

But it's Lulu's developing abilities to express herself verbally that I am continually in love with and in awe of. She can be charming or thoughtful or funny or grouchy or downright furious. And she can articulate every emotion in a range of words. She sings. She comments. She complains. She whines (boy, does she). She declares. She chatters. Constantly. I am watching a flower unfold before my very eyes. And although almost every child unfolds this way, she is my one and only flower, and so she is perfect.

Well, she is not perfect, but she is certainly perfectly herself. She has clear likes and dislikes, and she lets them be known.

"Ick! I do NOT like tomatoes!" or "Yum! I love pasta *con pesto!*"

She asks questions all the time.

"Mama, is it true that people cannot fly?"

"Yes," I said, "people cannot fly on their own."

Or...

"Mama, is it true that Daddy can fly?"

"Uhm, no, Daddy *cannot* fly," I answered wondering what may have prompted that one.

But, usually it's her quick observations or summations on what she sees and experiences in her life here in Italy that really send me over the moon.

I was taking her to school one morning when I was suddenly forced to bump her *passeggino* (stroller) down onto the street to go around a blue Fiat that had decided to straddle the sidewalk. *"Mi dispiace!"* ("I'm sorry!") the woman casually called over her shoulder, obviously not the least bit concerned that her parking spot had pushed a mother and child out on to the busy street. A cigarette between her lips, as she passed us, she flung it on the grass and sashayed inside.

"Italy is the place where everybody smokes and parks on the sidewalks," Lulu brightly summed up way too sharply for her age.

Even my Italian friends tilted their heads to one side, sheepishly shrugged their shoulders and nodded in agreement when I told them this. I've seen groups of teenagers, on some school field trip through Arezzo's historic center part of town, walking side by side with their teachers - and every one of them were lit up. A cigarette processional.

It was seeing those smoke-ringed adolescents that prompted me to realize that much more than the discomfort of constantly being on duty for an infant, it's the teenage-years I really fear. I survived the "taking" years, and now am reveling in the "give and take" years. But I am nervous about the impending "get away from me years." I know Lulu doesn't see it that way. Right now, Lulu does makes the distinction between "big kids" and "teenagers" but mostly, I think for her, those two separate stages are combined in her mind as one giant step into the vague distant future where she often envisions the nature of our relationship will be exactly the same as it is now.

For instance, Lulu said to me this morning as I was on the rug doing pushups, "But why are you doing that?"

"To keep my arms strong," I said.

"Great, so you can keep holding me even when I'm a teenager."

Lulu doesn't imagine that there may come a time when I won't be able to hold her. But I imagine that it won't have anything to do with her larger size. It will be more about her attitude. That rebel cool-factor, or whatever it is, that seems to infect us between twelve to eighteen and makes us do crazy things.

Like, for example, painting a seemingly never-ending, obnoxious stream of graffiti on the playground equipment at the hilltop park in Arezzo where we spend almost every afternoon after school. *Parco il Prato* is nestled between the town's Medici-built fortress and its cathedral, or *duomo*. It's dotted with pine trees and showcases a large marble stature of Arezzo's founding fathers including the father of Humanism, Petrarch, who was born here. It's also blanketed in a growing cover of spray-painted defacement that never gets painted over. Lulu likes to point out each new arrival as it appears on the slide or the swings.

"Who did that one, Mama?" Lulu asks.

"Naughty teenagers," I always answer. And although I can't know for certain, I don't think there's a gang of seven-year-olds out there prowling public parks at night. I can't imagine any adults doing that, either.

We're too busy taking care of our kids. So it must be teenagers. And the phrases they write are usually naughty. Most are in Italian. Some are in English. And some are in not very good—but very funny—English. My favorite is the "My *cook* is BIG" inscription on a bench near the cafe in the center of the park. I didn't think the size of one's, er, *cook*, was supposed to matter.

"I don't want to be a naughty teenager, Mama," Lulu always says.

"I don't want you to be one either," I always say.

So, while Lulu would like to grow up to one day have high heels and non-plastic jewelry of her own, she has decided that she isn't that keen on the growing-up thing itself.

She asked me one of her now-infamous "Mama, is it true...?" questions, while we were walking to the park after school one day. It's a question that always starts with "Mama, is it true?" and which almost always isn't. So, here was this one.

"Mama, is it true...?" she began.

"Yes, Lulu?" I inquired.

"Is it true that if you don't eat, you will still grow up?" she finished.

"Well, you need to eat some kind of food, I suppose, or you will just die after a while," I said, wondering where in the world this one was coming from.

"Well, Matilde at school told me that she is not eating anymore because she doesn't want to grow up and I don't want to either. Maybe if I just eat a little bit, I will only grow up only a little bit," she said.

Later, it was sometime around the week of her fourth birthday, and I had forgotten how Lulu wasn't completely enthusiastic about this aging business. I was trying to get her excited about her big day, telling her how happy I was that she was going to be getting another year older and how excited Mommy and Daddy were that she was "growing up," when something new crossed her mind.

"I'll still be your daughter, right?" she asked, her voice wavering.

"Of course, sweetie, you'll always be our daughter," I reassured her.

"But when I grow up, I have to move out of your house!" Now Lulu began to cry. She clutched her ever-present teddy bear friend, Vincent, close to her.

"If you don't want to move out, you don't ever have to," Scotty said. ("Oh, yes, she does," I thought, but did not say aloud.) Our verbal reassurances, however, were not working.

"I don't waaant to be big," she bawled. "Because I'm small now and you love me."

The next day she presented me with a piece of paper with one of those drawings of hers that seemed to get nicer and more detailed all the time. In magic marker, there stood a little yellow-haired girl surrounded by purple, pink, and orange flowers. The sun was smiling from one corner of the page and so was the girl.

"I drew a picture of me today," Lulu said handing me the sheet. "So when I grow up you will remember me."

Happily, a few days later, by the time her Hello Kitty cake was brought out and everyone was gathered around to sing *"Tanti Auguri a Te"* (which literally translates to "A Lot of Wishes for You" and is sung exactly to the tune of "Happy Birthday to You"), Lulu seemed to have forgotten her depression. Italian neighbors and friends were gathered around a large table on our patio. It was the end of November, but the sun was shining on the cypress trees and the weather was brisk but not too cold. We passed around slices of cake and poured orange juice for the kiddies and *prosecco* for the grownups.

We raised our glasses and sang. Lulu leaned over and blew out all the candles in one breath. She beamed about beginning year four. We seemed to have weathered the aging storm for now, but I couldn't help wondering how she'd fare turning forty.

◆　◆　◆　◆　◆　◆　◆　◆　◆

*"When I am a teenager, I would like some
lovely BRACELETS on my teeth."*

◆　◆　◆　◆　◆　◆　◆　◆　◆

TWO

HURLING INVECTIVES

* * * * * * * * * * * * *

A PEACE AND QUIET DINNER WOULDN'T BE ONE WITH LULU

ONE THING YOU CAN always count on if you have a toddler or a preschooler is that they will throw a tantrum or twelve. But what you can never be sure of is when or where the blessed events will occur.

When Lulu was only nine months old, with barely two teeth in her head, we were in the living room at my mother's home in Indiana. Crawling, Lulu managed to wrestle a mouse toy away from Snowflake, one of my mom's two very gentle and even baby-friendly cats. She then shoved the thing into her little mouth and began to use it as a teether.

"Gross," I said, as I yanked it out. "Lulu, that's dirty, honey. No, no. Icky."

Lulu stared up at me with the extracted "teether" in my hand.

"Oh, oh," my mother said, looking down at Lulu with

her wiser, experienced eyes. This woman had given birth to me, Andrea, and Brad, and then raised us largely alone after Dad died. When she married Jerry eight years later, she added his son, Jayson, into the mix. Each of us four kids had presented our own unique, uhm, *personalities* that she had to deal with. In Mom's chosen career before she retired, she had been a teacher of hearing impaired children, specializing in birth up to three years old. So, in short, this is a woman who knew a thing or two about kids and all the crazy things they can do.

I had never once diapered a baby before Lulu came along. I was an amateur. Mom was a seasoned professional. "I think you might've grabbed that too quickly from Lulu," she said. "Look at her face."

Mom was right, of course. In a flash, Lulu's face scrunched up like she'd sucked a whole lemon instead of a slimy, hair-covered cat toy. Her tiny eyes shut and her mouth, now free from impediments, opened wide. An animal howl came out. And then, what happened next I totally did not expect. Lulu, in one quick motion, hurled herself backwards, slamming flat onto the floor.

Luckily, we were sitting on a rare section of carpet, as a lot of Mom and Jerry's house is covered in hard stone tile. I stared at my child. She was lying on her back, arms and legs waving fiercely in the air, screaming as loudly as she could. A shrieking bug. My mom was watching all of this too, with interest. "Oh, Gina," she said, "you are going to have your hands full. None of you kids ever did something like that when you were that little."

Really? Could that be true? Oh no. None of us? Not even Andrea? I mean, she had had a great temper when she was a kid. Oh, man. What have we gotten ourselves into? I scooped up my little demon seed and began rocking and cooing to her to try and help her calm down.

When Scotty and I moved to Paris just a couple of weeks later, our small studio apartment was entirely covered in wall-to-wall head-splitting terracotta tile. We asked the landlords for a carpet and they gave us a thin Oriental rug—hardly enough to prevent brain trauma in case of another Lulu "episode."

Fortunately for her skull, Lulu instinctively understood the hard floor would hurt her. That's not to say she refrained from having "freak outs" as we began calling them, but that now, when the mood struck her, Lulu would first lower herself gingerly and carefully into proper recumbent position, and then commence her wailing and flailing routine.

Her private shows were going so well that one evening she decided to audition before the Parisian public.

Île Saint-Louis is the smaller of the two islands set in the Seine River. Its big sister, Île de la Cité, boasts Notre Dame, but I prefer the charm of Saint-Louis. The island is crammed full of tiny tranquil *patisseries,* boutiques, and cafes. There's a sort of doll-house scale to the size of all these shops, and my American friend Jane and I had zeroed in on a quaint *crêperie* that looked especially cute for an early dinner. In spite of the time, the place was already packed with patrons munching on their delicate crepes. We were squeezed into a table near the front door with Lulu sitting in her own "big girl" chair to my right. Jane smiled across at us, and we picked up our menus and began to get comfortable.

Jane and I originally met each other at a lovely French conversation group get-together. Although she didn't live in Paris full-time like we did, she split so much of her time between it and Boston that she probably accumulated more days in her visits than we eventually totaled during our continued stay. She and I had a lot in common. We both spoke amicable, if not perfect, French and we both loved exploring the City of Light. Together, with Lulu in tow, we visited museums, parks, and tea shops. But until tonight, we had never tried a dinner.

Jane ordered a crepe with chicken and I opted for the apple. Lulu decided to go for her glass of water. Clunk. Floosh. "Waaaah!" Her clasp attempt managed to knock the glass over—spilling water all over the white tablecloth. "No, Lulu, use two hands, honey." At least, I thought, the glass hadn't fallen onto the floor and shattered. It hadn't occurred to me to take a sippy cup along and, of course, no Parisian café would stoop to plastic, so we'd have to just try again. The waitress brought over another small glass and this time, I helped Lulu drink.

I hoped all was well and looked up at Jane. Her face had those raised eyebrows and that forced sort of smile that instantly tell you all is most definitely NOT well. "Maybe it's a little late for her," she said.

"Gosh, I hope not, she did have a nice nap," I said.

I handed Lulu a piece of baguette and she began to gnaw at it. Our dinners arrived and we managed to begin a bit of conversation. Then Lulu's nub of bread tumbled out of her hand and onto the floor.

"WAAAH!" Lulu cried as she reached down for it.

"No, Lulu, that's dirty. No. No," I said.

I don't know if I my words triggered visions of the icky mouse-shaped cat toy or what, but Lulu then and there decided to replay that scene. She couldn't throw herself directly from her chair to the floor, so first she climbed down from her perch descending onto my lap. Then she managed to writhe out of my grasp in the tightly packed little restaurant and slither under the table. She lay down on her back. Her hands and legs began to fly around in all directions. She began to scream. LOUD-LY. The other patrons sitting all of six inches away from us had no choice really but to stop and stare. Jane's eyes were bugging with incredulousness. I had to practically twist my body like a circus contortionist to get under that table far enough to wrestle Lulu out from there. I grabbed her.

I swept her up and out. Thank goodness we had been seated near the door. There was no dessert. No coffee. No nothing. I don't even remember paying. All I remember is my profuse apologies to Jane.

Did I forget to mention the one thing that Jane and I did not have in common? She had never had a child. Not even nieces or nephews. Jane had never experienced a toddler freaking out at her home. Certainly not in a crowded Paris café. But then again, neither had I, and that freak out was of epic proportion.

So it turns out Mom was more than right. Lulu was very likely a "spirited child"—meaning her emotions could be extremely intense and persistent. To put it in not-so-politically-correct terms, she could sometimes be an outright pain in the patookus. But thankfully, these days, for about eleven out of twelve hours, Lulu is a lovely freak-out-free little girl. She usually plays well with her friends at school, regularly picks up her own toys and clothes, and is mostly politely behaved in cafes. When she does become upset about something, she can now use her words to help express her emotions.

Like that morning last winter when it was only 5:30 a.m. and still pitch dark out. I woke up to the sound of Lulu in her room yelling.

I rushed in to see what was wrong and there she was on the floor, blessedly sitting upright, not flat on her back. She was wearing the pajamas she had slept in, but she had obviously gotten her new shoes out of her closet and put them on her bare feet. She was trying furiously to Velcro them closed.

"My shoes not right!! I freakin' out!!" she kept repeating. She began to kick and flail in a full meltdown, but I liked that she recognized it for what it was. It seemed to help her get a handle on it and calm down much faster.

Her words also help her express her other high-octane emotions like desire, although not always in the most polite terms.

"Get me on your lap!" she has demanded on more than one occasion.

One morning before school Lulu was adamant about what outfit she wanted to wear and with what accessories.

"If you do not get me my red hair bows I will never love you anymore and I will not play dolls with you."

"Lulu, you don't need to threaten me, just ask me nicely for something," I said.

"You mean I should say 'Please' and not, 'Put that barrette in now, if not, I will break your head off, just for pretend?'"

"Uhm, yes, that is exactly, sort of, kind of, a little bit like what I mean," I said.

Her floor falling has finally appeared to have fallen by the wayside and has now been replaced with a variety of colorful Lulu epithets. One memorably great tirade went this way (although for the life of me, I can't recall what triggered it.):

"I'm not your daughter anymore!" Lulu began. "I don't love you!"

"Luluuu," I cautioned.

"I only love Daddy!" she continued.

And then, as if she must thought that that last one didn't pack quite enough of a punch, she added, "Garbage! Banana Peel!"

I honestly have no idea where she came up with "banana peel" other than it's something she has to throw into the garbage, so, like "garbage," it must denote something dirty and icky. But anyway, I was pretty impressed. She'd come up with something original, besides simply flinging out an old standard like "meanie" or "dummy."

I figured nothing could top the Banana Peel insult until the next time around when Lulu was in the middle of a very similar rant. She was sitting on her bed in her room glaring at me about something and had just hollered out the "Garbage! Banana Peel!" zingers, when I saw her eyes dart across her room to her guest bed, on which sat a nest of stuffed animals. She searched for inspiration, singled out her favorite teddy bear "Vincent," and tossed out her newest epithet.

"...banana peel...and, and...Talking Bear!"

"Talking Bear?" I asked, giggling. "Why did you say that one?"

"Because," she began to giggle, too, "if Vincent really started to talk, I think that would be super scary."

I heard a child psychologist say that spirited children are like Model T Fords with jet engines inside. They just can't handle all that energy. But, the doctor added, those children should be able to eventually develop a firm handle on their extra energies and emotions and learn how to correctly channel them.

By the time they get to college.

◆ ◆ ◆ ◆ ◆ ◆ ◆ ◆ ◆

(During a particularly tense moment when she was acting up)

ME: *"Lulu, if you don't stop, you will lose an opportunity."*
LULU: *"That's okay, Mama, because you often forget."*

◆ ◆ ◆ ◆ ◆ ◆ ◆ ◆ ◆

THREE

VINCENT
• • • • • • • • • • • •
YOU'LL NEVER FORGET YOUR FIRST LOVE—
ESPECIALLY IF THE SECOND IS EXACTLY THE SAME

O F THE MULTITUDE OF STUFFED ANIMALS Lulu has, Vincent is by far her favorite. She has had that tan-colored, one-eared teddy bear with black eyes since she was just a month old. Scotty's dad, Grandpa Dan, brought it for her when he and Nana Kandie, Scotty's mom, came to visit after Lulu was born in Denver.

"You know I can't sleep without my Vincent," Lulu said to me last night. "I hug him so tight, he makes my eyes close. He is my one special Vincent."

That's what Lulu thinks. In fact, she's had *three* tan-colored, one-eared teddy bears with black eyes since she was just a month old. Because we keep losing them.

The first time was most tragic. Not for Lulu. For me.

It was Paris, Lulu was two and I had a lunch date with a lovely friend whom I hadn't seen in a while. Cynthia was one of the first anchors I wrote for when I just was starting out in television news. I was a lowly overnight writer at the Fox affiliate in Washington, D.C., and she was the statuesque, blonde news presenter. She was not only gorgeous; she was also funny and kind. I looked up to her like you would the coolest girl in school whom you could never even hope would be your friend.

Well, after a decade or so, I had had my own successful career as a TV anchor and correspondent, and Cynthia and I had indeed become friends and kept in touch. She was visiting Paris for a week, and wouldn't it be nice if we could meet for lunch? *Bien sûr!* The last time I saw her I had been pregnant, so I was eager to show off little Lulu.

Lulu didn't go anywhere without Vincent. He had earned his name, by the way, when he was mauled by our puppy Snoopy just a couple of months after Grandpa Dan brought him. Vincent had lost an ear in the attack, and I officially christened him in honor of the ear-mangled painter Mr. Van Gogh. Lulu didn't know any of the back-story at this time, of course; she just called out for him by name, "Wincent!" Well, almost by name.

So I placed Vincent with Lulu into her *pousette* (stroller) and walked over to the Commerce Metro Station by our apartment to take it to the Saint-Germain-des-Prés neighborhood where Cynthia was staying. Lulu clutched her inseparable best friend to her little bosom and I trundled away.

We arrived at Cynthia's hotel just as Lulu was deciding that she would rather nap than welcome and entertain a new guest. I greeted Cynthia with a hug and she peered in at Vincent and the drowsy Lulu. "Oh, she's so cute!" she said, "And, ha! Her bear only has one ear!"

"I know," I laughed, "we used to have a puppy that mistook Lulu's bear for one of its toys and chewed the ear right off. We now call him Vincent. The bear, not the dog."

I lowered the canopy at the top of Lulu's stroller to help shade her head as we rambled around a few blocks chatting and peering into the windows of the various art galleries that fill the streets of this labyrinthine *quartier*. We reached La Palette Bistrot on Rue de Seine for our lunch, and I parked Lulu and her stroller next to my chair by our table outside. I knew she was sound asleep, so I didn't bother to look in. Cynthia and I must've been there for more than an hour when I finally heard Lulu stir and leaned over to take a peek.

"Gasp!" The sound I made was that quick intake of breath you make when you're completely taken by surprise by something you suddenly see. Or, in this case, what I suddenly *didn't* see. Lulu was just fine, eyes still tightly shut, and snuggled a little bit on her side. But, Vincent was gone. Gone.

I sputtered out a rushed explanation to Cynthia what must've happened. Somewhere along our winding walk to the bistro Vincent had fallen from Lulu's sleep-filled limp arms and tumbled out. Because the stroller's awning-canopy-thingy-whatever-it's-called was up and blocking my vision, I hadn't noticed. As a mother herself, Cynthia was immediately sympathetic. We paid our bill and began to try to retrace our steps.

This is where I began to feel like a failure as a mother. Lulu would wake up from her nap and her practically life-long companion would not be there. Because I hadn't paid attention. Because I was too busy blathering with a friend to notice what was going on with my daughter. I should've known better. Especially since this had *almost* happened before. Déjà vu.

It was during another time in the same Saint-Germain-des-Prés neighborhood. Lulu had fallen asleep in her stroller again, and I had lowered the canopy to shield her from the day's bright sun. I then meandered through the narrow streets gazing in gallery display windows lost in thought. When I finally noticed Vincent had fallen out, I backtracked carefully through the alleys and passages—and this time I found him! Someone had been kind enough to lift him from the sidewalk and prop him on a low stone wall near the passage Cour du Commerce. I saw him sitting there on the wall in his floppy droopy-head style with three tourists crowding around taking photos of him. I could imagine the photo caption *"Lost Bear in Paris."* Lulu, who just then awakened, instantly saw him and cried, "Wiiin-cent!"

Those three same tourists then took photos of a joyful reunion between a little girl and her adored stuffy. *"Found Bear in Paris."*

But not so this day. Cynthia and I walked and walked and we walked some more. And we just couldn't find him. I was heartbroken. I had not only failed Lulu, but I had failed Vincent, too. I imagined him like a little living thing—all forlorn and lonely and afraid in a big city like Paris. He would never see Lulu again. I tried not to cry.

So much for our cheerful reunion. I trudged back with Cynthia to her hotel and she told me to wait outside. Lulu was just waking up and had already begun whimpering, "Wincent." "Wincent?" Cynthia quickly reemerged with a brand new stuffed animal that she purchased at the hotel gift shop. It was a sparkling white fluffy puppy and a very thoughtful gesture. I thanked Cynthia through my disappointment and handed it down to Lulu. She hugged it but then she looked up at me again. "Wincent?" she asked.

I understood. It just wasn't the same. Although new, bright, and white, the puppy couldn't compare to the dingy, tan, matted fur of beloved old one-eared Vincent. I said goodbye, thanked Cynthia again, and we returned home.

In our apartment, I whispered the sad story to Scotty while Lulu tried to play with her new toy on the carpet in the living room. She fuzzied the puppy's furry body to her cheek half-heartedly. Scotty calmly got up from the couch and walked over to the closet. He shuffled around to reach behind a few things on the top shelf and pulled out an opaque plastic bag. I had nearly forgotten! Scotty, smart father that he was and is, had the foresight to procure an identical teddy bear from the U.S. to take with us in Paris—just in case. And here was the case. This Vincent, however, had non-matted fur and *two* perky ears. Scotty disappeared into the other room where he carefully detached the "extra" ear and sewed up the incision with needle and thread. He then handed it over to Lulu telling her that he had taken the bear to the laundromat while she was napping to be cleaned and fluffed. Classic. I think Lulu may have initially suspected something, but she held it, hugged it, and buried her head in its fluffy fur. We were back in Vincent-action.

I have never felt guilty for pulling a fast-one on Lulu. I believe we were trying to ensure that a constant sense of comfort for her remained, well, constant. She loved Vincent and she preferred his presence over any other blanket, stuffed animal, or whatever. I still felt sorry for the original Vincent out there somewhere. I posted to my Facebook friends about the loss of Vincent and many responded by sharing similar heart-tugging tales of when their children had lost a favorite toy. My friend Christy even posted Don McLean's "Starry Starry Night" ballad in tribute of the loss of the real Vincent. I teared up as I listened.

For the remainder of our stay in Paris, I liked to imagine that Vincent the First managed to take up residence at the top of the Eiffel Tower and kept watch over Lulu, and all the other little children from above, like a teddy bear angel.

From that moment on, I kept a sharp eye on Vincent Number Two. I didn't lose him until more than a year later when we were living in Arezzo. For me, I guess that's pretty good, considering that Lulu doesn't leave our house without him. When we leave someone's house to come back to ours, it's critical I make a routine "Vincent check" before exiting. The one time I forgot to do that, we had walked all the way back from my friend Paola's house and it was bedtime before Lulu (and then I) noticed he was missing. Disaster.

With Lulu whimpering in the background, I called Paola and told her the news. She was on her way out the door to one of her many fancy dinner parties, but she graciously dropped everything and searched until she found him. Then she went out of her way to drop Vincent off to the great relief of his sleepy owner.

That was a close call. But there was bound to be another official loss and the second was almost just like the first—except in Italy now, not in France. Once again, Lulu fell asleep, canopy went up, and then again somehow, somewhere—*whoosh*. Vincent Number Two disappeared just like Vincent the First. And just like before, I looked all over the places where we had been. This time, though, I had to retrace steps through the Tuscan countryside, not Parisian streets. I jostled the stroller along a grassy path through a vineyard and I bumped over cobbled alleys. The routes may have been a little harder to navigate, but my heart this time was much lighter. We had been through this drill before. And again as before, Scotty was prepared.

I called him on his cell and he surgically prepped Vincent Number Three, which he again had purchased in the U.S. to take with us to Italy as back-up. He met us at Caffé dei Costanti in Arezzo's historic center of town. Lulu and I were there sitting at the counter happily snacking and waiting since I had already spun our cover story of "Daddy took Vincent to get cleaned up while you were sleeping." Vincent Number Three arrived "washed and fluffed" and—except for the appropriately missing ear—good as new. Because, of course, he was.

Lulu went to sleep that night snuggling with Vincent. "He smells so clean and cozy and fresh now, Daddy," she said as we tucked her in. "Thank you for washing him."

Scotty got on the computer to order Vincent Number Four in preparation for the next misadventure. But then the truly unthinkable happened. The small boutique store where Scotty's dad had first acquired Vincent (which was actually Walmart) no longer carried this kind of teddy bear. Oh no! If I lost Vincent Number Three, now I really would be a failure as a mother, because we wouldn't be able to make him magically reappear fresh and clean.

I was disheartened. Scotty was undaunted. He searched on-line in other Walmarts around the country. He inquired in separate on-line children's gift-shopping sites. He even went on Ebay. And that's where he discovered an exact little tan teddy bear for auction. For about *four times* as much as it had cost in the store. But considering that this was likely the last Vincent on the face of the planet, we forked over the price and now Vincent Number Four is here in Arezzo, tucked away and hidden high up on a closet shelf, wrapped in protective plastic. Scotty was even more proactive than the two previous times and has already deftly removed Vincent Number Four's left ear. Lulu probably wouldn't be particularly concerned about which ear is missing. She only cares that she has her Vincent bear with her every second.

And again he is. He's accompanying her to school and to the park and to bed. And he's back to his well-loved, scruffy-looking, regular old self. Maybe Vincent Number Two took the train from Italy and has joined Vincent the First atop the Eiffel Tower. I'll never know. All I know is that Lulu has a version of Vincent with her that makes her happy. And that makes me happy.

As I tucked her into bed, she cuddled her bear once again and said, "I love Vincent. I will love him forever."

◆ ◆ ◆ ◆ ◆ ◆ ◆ ◆ ◆

"Give me and Vincent a piggy-BANK ride."

◆ ◆ ◆ ◆ ◆ ◆ ◆ ◆ ◆

FOUR

THE LANGUAGE OF
CATS AND DOGS
* * * * * * * * * * *
I SPEAK ITALIAN BETTER THAN YOU!

ONE OF THE MOST INTERESTING challenges of living overseas is, not surprisingly, the difference in language.

Here in Italy, my communications skills are getting better. I can now make rudimentary sentences just like an American Tarzan. "Me want espresso." And I understand basic responses like, "Would you like sugar with that?" But it's just so frustrating when a fluent Italian speaker earnestly tries to express to me something a little more complex, and I simply cannot understand.

I'm not talking about the locals. I mean Lulu.

The girl is absolutely fluent. With a four-year-old's vocabulary perhaps, but in full sentences and with full speed. I am in awe when I listen to her now. Driving with her to swimming lessons this spring was the first time I vividly recall *hearing*, but not *understanding*, her.

Since we don't have a car here in Italy (our funds being very limited, buying and insuring a car is just impossible), we were with Lulu's best friend Allegra and her mom Michela. Allegra is a *bambolina* (cute little doll). The two are practically inseparable at school and their teachers describe the girls as *amiche del cuore*, or "friends of the heart." A lovely saying. Knowing the girls' fondness toward each other, Allegra's *mamma* invited me to enroll Lulu in swim lessons together with Allegra at the Chimera Nuoto, Arezzo's community pool.

This is no simple invitation. The swim center is a few kilometers outside the center of town—waaay out of walking distance for us *senza una macchina* (without a car). With bi-weekly lessons, Michela is committing to chauffeur us to and from swim lessons every Tuesday and Friday. That's quite an undertaking and Michela has been great about it, even trying to help me with my Italian during the drives. You might think then, what with the drive-time I spend in the front seat with Michela combined with my time spent hanging out with all the other parents at the coffee/wine bar in the waiting area at the pool during lessons, my Italian should be getting pretty good. But it's not enough to keep up with Lulu. (By the way, I'm not joking about there being a coffee/wine bar at the Chimera. We *are* in Italy.)

So, we're in Italy. We've been here for eight months now. And Lulu is fully immersed in Italian preschool for five hours every weekday. I should've seen it coming. But I just hadn't realized how much progress she had made until that day I heard her in the back seat seriously chatting with Allegra. They were jabbering (and giggling) so rapidly, I was astounded that I did not understand a single thing. It's a strange situation to hear your own child obviously having a wonderful conversation with a friend, and yet you're left completely in the dark. And not because they're whispering or conspiring, but simply because they're speaking a language you don't comprehend. Everyone told me how easily little children can pick up a second language, but to actually see and hear Lulu in action was, and still is, a marvel.

It was all white noise for me, when suddenly, as the swimming pool route took us past their preschool, the girls spontaneously yelled out in unison: "*Ciao, scuola puzzolente!*" I knew this must mean something significant to them because they then both burst out in riotous laughter. Michela, behind the wheel in the front seat immediately smiled at them in the rear-view mirror, shook her head and also laughed. I imitated her and tried to laugh in the same way as if to say, "Yeah, I agree with what you're laughing about." But I was acutely aware that I had no idea. Okay, I guess I had an inkling. I mean, I did understand the ubiquitous salutation "*ciao*" and I knew "*scuola*" meant "school." But for the last word, "*puzzolente*," which was clearly the key to unlocking the sentence, I had not a clue.

At home, after the lesson, I turned on the laptop and plugged the phrase into Google Translate. I unlocked it. The girls had said, "Hi, stinky school!" I smiled and rolled my eyes. All that for just this. Nice.

When we lived in Paris, my language skills in French weren't much better than now in Italy, but then, neither were Lulu's. The two years we were there happened to coincide with only Lulu's first and second birthdays, so she wasn't speaking much of anything, let alone French. I even felt that with my slight head-start from high school I would manage to stay a bit ahead. (However, I admit my French teacher had been from Wisconsin, so I had learned to say, "*Je m'appelle Gina*" with an upper Midwest, almost Canadian-like, flat accent, rendering the few phrases I remembered by the time we moved to France really of no use.) After my Parisian friends beat my accent into proper submission, I felt confident I was knowledgeable enough to teach my one-year-old daughter a few things in the local language.

"*Doucement, doucement, attention pour ta tête*" ("Careful, careful, watch out for your head"), I would caution as she climbed the playground monkey bars.

When she was with other children in the sandbox, "*Ne jette pas le sable*" ("Don't throw sand"), I would admonish.

Or, "*Viens ici, c'est l'heure de partir*" ("Come here, it's time to go"), I would call out when we had to leave the park.

Yes, virtually all the French I learned during our stay was related to playing at the park or parenting. I couldn't speak to anyone about *fois gras* or fine champagne but I could talk all day about *les biberons* (baby bottles), *les couches* (diapers), and *les tétines* (pacifiers). Perfect conversation starters for little Lulu.

"*Où est ton biberon* (Where's your bottle)?" I could ask Lulu and she would toddle off to retrieve it. She also knew how to correctly respond to the French equivalent of "What does a (insert any animal here) say?" And when she was hungry she knew precisely how to plaintively cry, "*J'ai faim, maintenant, Maman!*" with that perfect, ear-splitting, upward inflectioned whine like every demanding French (or otherwise) toddler. But that was about it. I was a little worried since Scotty and I mostly spoke English to her that Lulu would be confused, which would delay her development in either language. I would be able to help in English, but I really couldn't tell in French.

I looked to my friend Dana for guidance. She was one of my dearest *copines* in Paris with an adorable, curly dark-haired son named Alec who is a year older than Lulu. The two played together in almost every park in Paris and had a remarkable friendship. Dana listened to Lulu's baby French alongside the supreme fluency of Alec's. "Relax. She's really doing great," Dana reassured me. "Her French sounds just like Alec's did when he was only two."

When we re-entered the U.S., Lulu was nearing three years old and chattering away. The teachers at her new preschool in Baltimore were enchanted by how she spoke. Dogs were *chiens,* Cats were *chats,* and a butterfly in the school's courtyard was a *papillon.* When she was done eating at lunchtime, Lulu said *"fini"* instead of "finished." When she was expressing her terrible twos, she stamped her foot and declared, *"Je ne veux pas ça!"* ("I don't want that!")

In fact, even though her skills were really extremely basic, Lulu's French bested all her American teachers, prompting them to ask me to make a little notebook of French words and phrases to help better understand her.

I hired a French tutor for me to preserve what little of the language I had learned for both Lulu and my sakes. I also joined a French oriented playgroup, *Le Petit Groupe Français,* so Lulu could be around other American children speaking French to encourage her to continue with the language. Unfortunately, *le groupe* was geared more toward non-working moms, holding most of its playdates on week days when I was at my job and Lulu was surrounded by little English speakers at Baltimore's Bolton Hill Nursery. I even tried taking Lulu to the only French bakery in town, Napoleon's in Fell's Point on the harbor, for our adored French treat of *pain au chocolats.* Looking at all the beautiful things behind the glass counter, I excitedly ordered our treats in French. The teenage girl at the register stared back at me and said, "Huh? Whadju you say?" That didn't sound much like Paris. The pastries didn't taste like Paris either.

By the time, almost a year later, that we had decided to move back to Europe, this time to Italy, only a few French remnants lingered in our regular repertoire. Lulu still called the living room the *salon.* A hot chocolate was still a *chocolat chaud.* And she still referred to her love-worn, one-eared teddy bear named Vincent, as her *dou-dou,* which literally translates as "soft-soft" and is what Parisian children adorably call their favorite stuffies. But that was about it.

Just days before we flew to Rome, we were at a cookout with some multi-lingual friends and their kids, and one of the dads leaned down to Lulu and asked her something in French. She smiled but didn't respond at all. "That's okay," he told me. "It's time to make way for Italian."

And it was true. Little by little (or *piano, piano* as the Italians like to say) her stroller, which was a *pousette* when we lived in Paris, became a *passeggino.* Our *maison* became a *casa.* I embraced the evolution. First, I began making up Italian words by adding an Italian-sounding ending to its Latin cousin French word. A couple of times I managed to get the point across like when I said *"vas avanci"* for "go forward" to a taxi driver.

It was an awkward mix of the French *vas* for "you go" and my made-up Italian ending to the French "forward," or *avance*. The real Italian word for "forward," by the way, is *avanti*. The Italian driver miraculously got my gist and smiled back at me for my effort. I was having fun. But, for Lulu, this idea of introducing a third language into her life in almost as many years was too much.

"Speak the language I speak!" she would holler at me when I tried out a new Italian phrase on her. She told me she missed her "English friends" in Baltimore. We sent post cards to her best friend Amelia. Her family sent cards and gifts back. We kept up with the goings-on of her old Bolton Hill Nursery gang through Facebook. At her new Italian preschool, even with its lovely lilting name *Bianca Maria Bianchini*, Lulu was mostly quiet and a little withdrawn.

In October, I thought we'd try a return visit to Paris to cheer her up. We went back to our old neighborhood park in the 15th *arrondissement,* Parc Georges Bressens (named for a wonderful Parisian folk-singer), with my cherished friend from our time there, Christiane. Lulu held Christiane's hand and re-explored her old surroundings. She actually seemed to recognize the playground climbing equipment and the large fountains with the ducks. We took in a *Polichinelle* puppet show at the small theatre nestled in the park. The puppeteer, Philippe, said he remembered us from a year ago when we were regulars and remarked how much Lulu had grown. We dropped by Lulu's fabulous *garderie* (daycare), La Ribambelle, where she was met with warm hugs by two of her previous favorite teachers, Bernadette and Rodolfo.

The best part was the reunion between Lulu and Alec. He and his family met us at Paris's historic amusement park, Jardin d'Acclimatation, which has been enchanting children since the time of Napoleon III. The kids rode the twirling tea pots, the bumper cars, even the roller coaster, *twice.* Lulu definitely was revived and restored. Alec spoke solely in French so Lulu broke out some of her rusty words, tossed in a few new Italian ones, and filled in the rest with English. It was a great day.

When we got home, Lulu was clearly invigorated by her cultural exchange experience. She happily returned to Bianca Maria Bianchini, and I decided it was better to leave it to the Italians to teach her their language. So, her classmates and *maestre* (teachers) helped Lulu with her Italian, and I switched to coaching her on speaking English better. I started working with pronunciation problems she had (in an encouraging way of course; Lulu was only a three-year-old, after all). She couldn't make that "consonant cluster," when you say the letter "s" plus any other consonant. She *could* make the "s" sound next to a vowel with no problem, but next to a consonant, not at all. Her Italian "*serpent*," for example, was perfect, while "snake" was just "nake."

It had been going on since back in Baltimore, when one winter's day as I drove her to Bolton Hill Nursery, it began to flurry. Lulu incoherently called from the back seat, "*Top* the car, Mama, it *nowing* now. I wanna play, not go to *cool*."

I helped her practice making the "s" sound alone and then adding in the remainder of the word. It was like a segment from the old children's TV show, The Electric Company.

"Sss." "Top." "Stop."

"Sss." "Nowing." "Snowing."

"Sss." "Cool." "School."

Lulu caught on quickly. Her English was really progressing. It was around the same time that I noticed her Italian usage was advancing too. Not only by the full sentence back-and-forths she was having with Allegra, but with other students, her teachers, our neighbors, everyone. She was even trilling her "r's" like a native. "*Guardami, Mamma*," or "Look at me, Mama," she would say with a perfect Italian "rrrrr." She was no longer demanding for me to "speak the language" she spoke, since now she spoke two. It was the opposite. One afternoon, as we passed some British tourists holding an English conversation, Lulu whispered to me, "Whenever we hear people talking English, Mama, let's talk in Italian. I love talking in Italian!" I would be happy to try, I told her, but she would have to help me because she had surpassed me. While I could teach her English, Lulu had become my little teacher, or *maestrina*, of Italian.

At a shop or café, when I needed help finding the right Italian word, Lulu was more than happy to chime in and help, but she often told the shopkeeper or server more than I bargained for.

"*Parlo meglio di Mamma.*" ("I speak bettter than Mamma.") And it's true. So last week, I thought I'd try another round of English pronunciation lessons. Lulu's latest hiccup has been in making the soft "th" sound. She says "free" instead of "three"; "fumb" instead of "thumb"; and "fing" instead of "thing." So I thought I would ask her to pronounce a series of words with that sound in order to practice saying them correctly. But she was too quick for me. This time I wasn't prepared for how much she'd accelerated, not only in langugage skills, but also in cunning. Our entire lesson went like this:

Me: Lulu, how do you say say "think?"

Lulu: *Pensa.*

Lulu inserted the Italian word for "think" and soundly beat me at my own game. She definitively showed me how much better children are at adapting to new linguistic surroundings than we are as adults. And then she took it even further.

"Mama, I am better'n you in speaking," she bragged. "I speak Français, English, and Italiano."

29

And if those weren't enough, she then added two more I was unaware of.

"And I also speak the language of cats and dogs."

Class dismissed.

◆ ◆ ◆ ◆ ◆ ◆ ◆ ◆ ◆

LULU: *"Reput my shoes."*

ME: *"You mean, 'Put my shoes back on.'"*

LULU: *"Okay. Reput my shoes back on."*

◆ ◆ ◆ ◆ ◆ ◆ ◆ ◆ ◆

FIVE

HAIR**STRAIGHT**DOWN

❖ ❖ ❖ ❖ ❖ ❖ ❖ ❖ ❖ ❖ ❖

LULU DOES NOT PRACTICE WHAT SHE PREACHES

L ULU IS FIXATED WITH the way I wear my hair. In short, she only likes it long. And she has an adorably pleasant way of expressing her preferred style to me. To better understand, read this coming up out loud at maximum volume and really, really fast, as one single word.

Ready?

Go: "HairStraightDown!"

It works something like this. I have just finished pushing Lulu in her *passeggino*, along with a couple of heavy bags full of groceries shoved into the basket underneath, for about an hour under the scorching Tuscan sun on the way home. Up the steep cobbled streets from the supermarket. Down the hill that leads us outside the walls of the city. Along the narrow shoulder of busy Via Buonconte Montefeltro street with its way-too-fast Italian drivers. Turning right onto the blessedly much quieter road Via della Cella. Past the vineyards. Past the wide meadow where the Count has his villa (we really do live near an honest-to-God Count). Between our neighbors' sprawling compound houses. Onto our *strada bianca* (gravel road). Past the wrought iron front gate and then finally through our door and into our home.

I am sweaty, grouchy, and tired. I kick off my shoes and reach for a clip to lift my damp hair from my neck.

The instant Lulu notices—like some weird Pavlovian response—she barks, "HairStraightDown!"

"Lulu," I say, helping her out of the *passeggino*. "Mommy's hair is bugging her and she just wants it up for a little bit."

"HairStraightDooown!" she repeats. This time the command is louder, sharper, and whinier.

"Lulu, Mommy is the same person no matter how her hair looks. I'm leaving it up for a moment while I unpack the groceries." I go for a diversion. "Want me to turn on the TV?"

"No!" she yells. "I want your HairStraightDoooown!!"

"Lulu," I say, "when you are quiet, I will turn on the TV. Would you like that?"

Undaunted, she is now chanting like a participant in some evil mob demonstration scene.

"HaairStraaightDooooown!"

"HaairStraaightDooooown!"

"HAAAAIRSTRAAAAIGHTDOOOOWN!"

I know that all children try to control and manipulate their parents at times. I just didn't realize it could be about something so arbitrary. We have a photo of Lulu from when she was an infant wearing a Napoleon hat that Scotty made for one of his performances. It feels like she is channeling the emperor right now. Or, maybe she's more Machiavellian. I have a fleeting thought to write a children's book detailing the lessons of cunning control from Niccolo Machiavelli through the eyes of a child. I'll call it, *The Little Prince*. Oh wait, that title is already taken and it's a much more enjoyable read. I snap out of my despot absorption and back into reality.

"Lulu, you do not dictate my hairstyle. That's enough," I firmly say. I realize she doesn't understand the word *dictate*, but I have little dictators on the brain now.

One of the articles I read about how to deal with your child's controlling issues, encourages parents to reassure the child that there are things she can control in her world and to remind her of those.

"Lulu, honey," I begin, "you can choose what program you would like to watch on TV. Let's turn it on and we'll see."

"Nooooo! I just want your *(here it comes again)* HAIR-STRAIGHTDOWN!"

Honestly, I don't know if I should pick my battles and acquiesce at this point, letting my stringy, sweaty hair just hang, or tell her to march into her room, where she will no longer be visually offended by my up-do, until I have the groceries put away and have had a chance to cool down.

I decide to go back to the "distraction TV solution," but I no longer try to engage her in conversation about whether she wants it on or not, or what program she would like to choose. I just walk over and snap on the TV set while she's in the midst of another bellow.

"HAIRSTRAIGHTDOOO…?"

She stops and turns.

Thank my lucky stars. The animated series of Mr. Bean happens to be on right now on the *Cartoonito* channel. I confess, I have never been a big fan of Rowan Atkinson, but now I would kiss him right on the lips. That's because for Lulu, Mr. Bean is her number one most *favoritist* thing on TV. She loves him. He has just shattered his mug with the picture of Queen Elizabeth on it. How will he ever get a new one? Lulu closes her mouth and turns to watch. My hair has been forgotten. I silently close the door to the kitchen, put the groceries away, and exhale. Whew.

What is especially frustrating about the big to-do over my hair-do is that Lulu has absolutely no sense of fairness. She insists that her own hair, which, like mine, would hang past her shoulders if "straight down," be pulled up into a high ponytail on top of her head. Mine must always hang loose, but not hers.

"Make me a fountain!" she proclaims. "My hair is itchin' my neck off."

She wears the fountain when she plays at home. She has a fountain when we go "out in the country," which is ironically how she describes when we go into the center of town (likely because we walk through so much rural countryside to get there). Lulu spouts a fountain at school. And lately she's even been asking for a fountain when she goes to bed.

"I don't like my hair movin' on my pillow," she explains.

I point out to Lulu that if she can wear her hair up, then Mommy should be able to do the same. I've already tried reassuring and distracting, so why not reasoning?

"But I just like your HairStraightDown. Your face looks prettier that way," she says.

I rolled my eyes.

When I was in Tunis and then Rome recently for a week of conducting media trainings, I called Lulu and Scotty every night around bedtime to check in. Scotty and I had been a little worried about how she might react to me being gone. It was the first time I had been away from Lulu for so long since the day she was born.

I first talked to Scotty and then he put Lulu on the phone. I had already bought her a fuzzy warm pair of slippers at a market in Tunisia, so I was prepared for the expected "did you get me a present" question. I had also mentally rehearsed the comforting things I would say when she said she missed me. But I swear to you the first words out of Lulu's mouth were, "Is your HairStraightDown, Mama?" I couldn't believe my ears. It was a little weird. Like a pint-sized variation of the cliché phone question to a lover who's far away, "Hey, what are you wearing?"

I couldn't get over it. Not my expected and prepared for topics like, "I miss you, Mama." Or, "Did you get me a present?" Just a question about my blasted hair.

I sighed and paused. Then I sweetly cooed into the phone, "Oh, Lulu, cutie. Why, of course, my hair is straight down."

"Okay, good, Mama. I love you when you are 'HairStraightDown,'" she said. "Good night, Mama. I love you and I miss you. You are a lovely Mama."

So, now little Lulu would go to bed happy with that comforting image of me with my HairStraightDown. But since we weren't on video phones, she would never know for sure if my hair really was or wasn't.

And I would never tell.

◆　◆　◆　◆　◆　◆　◆　◆　◆

"Everyday I'm your daughter, right?"

◆　◆　◆　◆　◆　◆　◆　◆　◆

SIX

SHOWDOWN AT STORY TIME
* * * * * * * * * * * * *
MY DAUGHTER IS A TURKISH CARPET DEALER

I'VE HEARD THE BEST WAY to encourage your child to enjoy reading as an adult is to read to them as much as you can while they are little. So, since Lulu was a baby, we have rolled out a steady stream of books.

The first were classics like *Runaway Bunny* and *Goodnight Moon*. In her nursery back in Denver, I would rock Lulu, holding her in my left hand close to my chest, clutching a book in my right hand, and raising it over her body so I could see. I would keep reading aloud until either she, or my outstretched arm, fell asleep. Whichever came first.

When we moved to Paris, we had to pack light so we couldn't take many books. We bought some new ones once we arrived, at a *librairie* on our block on Rue de la Convention. They were in French, naturally, and since they were written for children, they were also at the perfect reading level for beginning French-speakers like Scotty and me. One of our favorites was *Comme Cochons* (*Like Pigs*) by Soledad Bravi.

This card-stock, sturdy little book was bright orange with a drawing of two smiling mud-splotched little piggies standing upright, arm in arm. Each page inside featured an equally adorable drawing of an animal accompanied by a funny French idiom; the piggies, for example, were illustrating the French saying *"amis comme cochons,"* or "great friends like pigs."

While our French-speaking skills remained elementary at best, the book allowed us, at least, to leap ahead with colorful phrases you would probably never learn unless you were native-born or a very, very advanced student. When I gave Lulu her bath, for example, she wasn't just naked, now she was *"nu comme un ver,"* or "naked as a worm." I never understood our American English jaybird reference, anyway, so this was perfect. When she cried, she no longer cried like the baby she was; now she inexplicably cried *"comme une vache,"* or like a cow. I don't understand that idiom, unless the cow is particularly upset about being a cow. Which is probably not all that fun, considering *Steak Tartare*.

And when I mentioned to my Parisienne girlfriend, Laurence, that Elisa was *"bavard comme une pie,"* or "someone who gossips like a magpie," I don't know if Laurence laughed more from hearing me surprise her with a clever French quip, or from the fact that I had just made a not-so-nice crack about our mutual friend.

Here in Tuscany, we brought a couple of our French books with us, and family and friends have mailed us English stand-bys like *Frog and Toad are Friends* and every Disney story you can think of. We already have a few lovely Italian titles, too, including a book Lulu thinks is named for her, *Stella* (star) *Lulu* and, of course, the must-have for any Italian children's book collection: *Pinocchio*.

I will read to Lulu almost any time she asks me, but at night-time it's a requirement. Hers, not mine.

She'll call out, "One story, one song! Night, Night!" which is the way I have tried to frame bedtime in an effort to make it as expeditious a routine as possible. Sometimes by the end of the day, I would be grateful if she didn't want to hear any story at all, but rather chose to brush her teeth by herself, put on her own jammies, turn out her light, and tuck herself in. But that is definitely not how it goes. Instead it goes more like this:

At about eight o'clock, I make the first announcement.

"Lulu, it's eight o'clock so it's time for bed." Which, I know is really not ever actually the precise time she'll lay down in her bed, but merely signifies the beginning of our evening's countdown.

"Ma-maaa," Lulu always begins to whine. "Not yet! I'm not sleepy at all."

"Okay, Lulu." (Why do I always say this?) "I will give you five more minutes."

"But Mama-dear..." Lulu always counters. (Lulu has started tacking on "dear" to my name now as a means, I'm convinced, to really sock it to me with kiddie cuteness in her art of persuasion).

"How about eight more minutes?" (She also tries to replace my suggested "five" with "eight," instead of say, "ten" or "twenty" more minutes, because I swear she knows she has better chances in smaller increments.)

So, our nightly haggling session begins.

"Okay, Lulu, I will give you six," I say this, thinking she can't possibly tell the difference between five and six. "And then we're off to get jammies on and brush your teeth."

"Okay, Mama-dear," Lulus says.

I know I should not give in to her wheeling and dealing for any time delay at all. But she would throw a complete tantrum if I didn't give her some sort of advance warning. Which might prompt one to suggest that I should really start the countdown at 7:30, then, and that someone would be correct. But sometimes eight o'clock just sneaks up on me.

"How about seven minutes?" she suddenly asks, apparently realizing she missed a minute here and trying to split the difference. At least she's learning to count pretty well.

Scotty says this is about the time Lulu puts on her imaginary Turkish carpet dealer hat and prepares for real battle. Imagine you're in a covered souk baazar and little Lulu comes at you, bowing and wearing a red fez and offering you some green tea from one of her tiny porcelain tea set cups. I guarantee before you know what hits you, you will be leaving with a hand-knotted silk or wool rug. No question. She's that good.

"*Leesten, friend, have I got a deal for you,*" she would say. "*Seet here and drink this tea. Now leesten, friend, I just want to stay up just a leetle longer this evening. Only thees one time. It's not a precedent*—(Lulu seriously does know this word, because I have had so many occasions to use it with her)—*I promeese. You won't be sorry, friend. Just thees one time. Take eet. Take eet. Eet's a bargain. Only seven more minutes. Let me stay up.*"

"Lulu, all right, you may stay until the end of this next cartoon," I say (yes, yes, the TV is on), "but then it's really straight to bed." I know that this is probably even longer than her seven-minute bargain, but I figure seeing the credits roll at the end of *Baby Looney Tunes* (in Italian, of course) is tangible for her, whereas hearing me just call out the end of six or seven or whatever minutes is not—and would likely make for another round of time-bartering.

"Yes, Mama-dear," Lulu coos from the couch. The carpet dealer has won.

Scotty clicks off the TV as soon as *Baby Looney Tunes* is over, and I spring into action. Clothes off and pajamas on. (It's Europe, so no, we don't bathe every day anymore, what can I tell you?) Lulu stands at her "tiny sink" which is actually the bidet and holds her Thomas the Train battery-powered toothbrush to her mouth. By the way, all of the parents of Lulu's friends have bidets that are festooned with kiddie soap dispensers, sponges, toys and yes, even toothbrushes. It encourages her to want to brush more, since it's right at her level. And anyway, the bidet is not getting used for anything else. We're American, after all.

After she spits and rinses, we head into her bedroom and I think I'm finally in the homestretch. A few months ago, I imposed my supposedly delay-proof "one story, one song, night-night" rule that I mentioned. In theory, Lulu can pick out any story she wants from her stack of books, but only one, and then I will read it. But, that's it. No compromises. No negotiations. But, man, as I already told you, she's good. And now, she puts her imaginary red fez back on.

"I want *Corduroy*," she starts. "No wait, how many pages that story have? Maybe I want *The Little Girl Who Tried to Play with the Stars*. How long is that one?"

(*"Leesten, friend, I know it's just one book, but I theenk we should find the longest one. Here, drink a cup of this delicious mint tea."*)

"Lulu, honey, they all have approximately the same number of pages," I say. "Just pick one."

She decides to go for *Pinocchio*. This one is written in Italian and although it is blessedly an abridged version, she also knows it's by far the lengthiest. I begin to read.

"Mama," she interrupts only a couple of paragraphs in, "was I first born wooden as a baby?"

Here's a hurdle I haven't figured out how to clear. It's a delay-tactic disguised as an innocent question. It's a pretty funny one, too, so I give it a quick volley.

"No, of course not, honey, you were first born as a little monkey and we had to take you to the zoo veterinarian to have him snip off your tail."

She giggles, satisfied by that answer, so I get a few pages of *Pinocchio* under my belt before she starts a new strategy: correcting my Italian. It's true that being in preschool for five hours of Italian immersion everyday has made Lulu much more conversant than either Scotty or me, but I figure I should be doing all right with *Pinocchio* since I'm reading, not trying to form sentences on my own. However, Lulu the Carpet Dealer has figured another way to keep me in the souk, I mean, her bedroom, a bit longer, so she begins to interrupt—saying that I pronounced that word wrong there. Then there. And then that word, too.

"Okay," as I shut the book, not too abruptly I hope, "why don't we read something else? Something in English. How about *The Three Little Pigs*?"

She loves this book, especially because I do all sorts of goofy voice imitations when it comes to the dopey first and second little pigs, the extremely intelligent, but nerdy, third little pig, and of course, the notorious villain himself, the Big Bad Wolf.

I'm cruising along when the stalling begins again. Now she's moved into the tactic I'll call "detail clarification." "Are they brother pigs, Mama-dear?" she asks, opening her eyes as wide and as Puss-in-Boots cute as she possibly can. "Or are they just friends?"

"Lulu, I don't know. This story doesn't say. But, I do think there are some versions in which they are described as brothers." Why am I giving it this much thought? The tiny carpet dealer is clearly getting me to buy another *kilim*.

"Where does he get his straw, Mama-dear?"

"I have no idea."

"What kind of sticks? All kinds? Big ones or teeny tiny ones?"

"Lulu, just sticks, okay?"

I finally limp toward the first visit from the Big Bad Wolf and Lulu decides to offer her own detail clarification here.

"Mama, I think they call him BIG because he is ginormous. They call him BAD because he is naughty. And they call him WOLF because...well..." she pauses to think, then resumes, "well, I guess because he is a wolf."

Wow, that is deep. I find myself suppressing a laugh but it's obvious we're not going to finish this one anytime soon either. Lulu usually lets me breeze through *The Little Mermaid* (Disney's cheery version, not the depressing Andersen original), so I offer up this final book as a last-ditch attempt at completing a single story.

"Mama-dear," Lulu pipes up, "do mermaids exist in real life?"

Argh. I can already tell where this book is heading, too. Okay, so much for the one-story rule. I think Lulu the Carpet Dealer has wheeled and dealed me into reading about three of them tonight. If I squint, I think I can actually see her wearing that darn fez.

◆　◆　◆　◆　◆　◆　◆　◆　◆

    LULU: *You take care of everything*
               for me, Mommy. You take
               care of Daddy, too."
    ME: *Who takes care of me?"*
    LULU: *You do that also."*

◆　◆　◆　◆　◆　◆　◆　◆　◆

SEVEN

LIKE A PRAYER

* * * * * * * * * * * * *

WHEN LULU HAD A LITTLE TALK WITH GESU

LULU WAS ENTERING HER first Catholic Church. I was hoping like the devil she'd behave.

We were in Shelton, Washington, to celebrate the 90th birthday of Lulu's great-grandfather, "Pop-pop" Frank Walsh. His party, the day before, had been that family-reunion type of successful event. Adults clustered in groups chatting and gossiping while dozens of grand- and great-grandkids, many of whom had never met each other before, gorged themselves on ice cream and cake, colored cowboy and cowgirl mask favors, and generally screamed and ran around in everyone's way.

Now, in the quiet afterglow of that event, we were filing into Pop-pop Frank's church for Sunday morning service. Pop-pop was shuffling along slowly while Scotty's dad lingered back to assist his father. Scotty, holding Lulu in his arms, and I walked side by side. His mom was in front, leading us down the aisle and heading dangerously closer and closer to the front.

We ended up in the second row, ever so near the altar, the priest, and his assorted attendees. I worried that Lulu's every sniffle or shift in her seat might be a disturbance. It was so far so good, until the first time Scotty's mom innocently lowered the little prayer bench and Lulu's eyes opened wide. It was like a new toy had been delivered to the playground.

"What is *that*, Mama?" Lulu asked in a talking voice that was not at all at proper church-whisper volume.

"Shhhh!" I began, not daring to look up toward the priest and his entourage. "It's a bench for prayer."

I managed to keep her from hopping down and trying to toggle it back and forth incessantly, as she does with those not-quite-all-the-way-soldered-shut ashtrays that are still in the arms of many seats on older jets. Lulu finds them fascinating—which of course completely infuriates everyone else on the plane.

We settled on a compromise. She could hop down with Nana and Grandpa Dan during the kneeling times, if she behaved quietly during the in-between times. I was beginning to feel like we were going to make it, when the processional to take Communion commenced. Now people began actually getting up and out of their pews.

Here was some action. Lulu's eyes really lit up.

She eagerly watched the parishioners file past us on the way to take the sacrament from the priest. She told me she wanted to go "for a walk" too, but on this one, I wouldn't budge.

She kept craning her neck to better see what was going on and finally she couldn't take it anymore.

"What kind of chips they givin' out for their snack-time!?" she asked me, oh-so-embarrassingly audibly.

No one said a word at that moment, but on the way out of the building after service, my father-in-law turned to me and remarked, "Maybe you should take her to church more often."

During the first two years of Lulu's life in Paris, we visited both Notre Dame, the city's oldest Catholic Church, and its newest: the *Notre Dame de l'Arche d'Alliance* in our 15th *arrondissement* neighborhood. But we had never actually taken Lulu to a formal service.

The longest time Lulu had spent in a church was during part of her third year, when we were back in the States. Bolton Hill Nursery in Baltimore was housed in the upstairs Sunday school floor of a Protestant Church of which I no longer remember the official denomination. It was an enormously creative school with a curriculum that centered on teaching through art and performance. The teachers used the church basement as a rec room, where they held all sorts of activities and events. In the winter, it became a beach. Children were invited to wear their swimsuits and frolic in plastic wading pools filled with sand, plastic buckets, shovels, and sifters.

In the summer, the basement was the setting of a preschool version of Baltimore's famous annual "Hon Fest." (*Hon* is a take on the folksy way locals from Baltimore greet one another as in, "Hi ya, hon.") Hon Fest is a flamboyant festival that exaggerates Baltimore's folksiness—with big bee-hive hair-dos, leather jackets, and plenty of homage to hometown hero and dark-comedy film director, John Waters (who brought us such irreverent classics as *Pink Flamingos* and *Hairspray*).

Bolton Hill's church basement was transformed into a beauty salon with teachers spraying and teasing little girls' hair into up-dos and slicking the boys' hair and rolling up their short sleeved white T-shirts. They even had a Hon Fest variation of the pin-the-tail-on-the-donkey game: pin-the-pencil-thin-mustache on John Waters.

In the spring it was yoga. Every week, an instructor came to Bolton Hill and helped the little ones stretch and get flexible. Lulu loved it. I didn't realize just how much she loved it until her three-year-old check-up, when the doctor was examining her coordination and balance skills. She asked Lulu to try and stand on one foot. My daughter proceeded to lift up a foot, then wrap that foot's leg around the still standing leg, clasp her small hands in prayer position to her chest, and thereby create the yoga "Tree Pose."

"Well, isn't that something. I have never seen anything like it," said the doctor, shaking her head.

"Neither, have I," I said a bit dazed as Lulu continued to stand there before us, motionless. "I had no idea."

"Do you want me to show you 'Downward Dog' now?" asked Lulu. "That's what our teachers make us do when we need wiped after poo-poo."

At the Bolton Hill Nursery-School-in-a-Church, Lulu also learned her numbers and the alphabet. "'A' is for Amelia, 'E' is for Evan. 'J' is for Jasmina," Lulu would come home and say.

The children practiced manners during lunch and snack times. Clearly they had gone beyond the basics of where to place your napkin and how to hold your fork. One day after school, Lulu sat down primly at the dinner table with us and said, "Let's have a tiny conversation."

They took walks outside around the neighborhood, pointing out shapes. A door was a rectangle, the manhole covers were circles, and the stop sign when I was driving her back home was "an octopus."

Her year at the "church" in Baltimore was, to us, a wonderfully educational one, just not a very worshipful one.

Here in Italy, a country where the Catholic Church has dominated for millennia and the Pope is called simply *"Papa,"* worshipfulness is every -where. Lulu and I play the "find the Madonna" game as we walk to school every morning. Whoever discovers the most statuettes of the Virgin Mary that are nestled in small alcoves in houses, enshrined on the sides of the roads in altars, or painted in fresco and encased in the walls of shops and buildings, is the winner. Lulu has no idea about the pop-singer with the same name. But she sure knows *"Madonna, la Mamma del Bambino Gesu."*

One of the most famous religious relics here in Arezzo, in fact, is a Madonna. The *"Madonna del Conforto,"* or "Madonna of Comfort," is a small terracotta-painted plaque of the Virgin. Apparently, it was just hanging out in some basement hundreds of years ago when a series of earthquakes threatened to damage the city. A group of people huddled around the plaque and prayed. As legend has it, the Madonna suddenly began to glow and the tremors ceased.

Since then, it's been moved out of the basement, to a more prestigious location in an ornate chapel within the city's main cathedral, or *duomo*. Every February, there's a festival in the plaque's honor. Never one to miss out on a traditional festival, I packed Lulu up warmly and pushed her *passeggino* all the way into town. Inside the cathedral, the plaque was festooned with hundreds of white lilies. Candles were shimmering all over. We stood in the queue at the chapel, and when we arrived in front of the plaque, we were sprinkled with Holy Water from the priest.

"Was that magic water?" Lulu asked when we were back outside.

"Sort of, I guess," I said, figuring a complete explanation was not really what she was after.

"Now, can we get some candy?"

"Sure."

I brought her some assorted gummies from one of the carts waiting at the bottom of the cathedral's steps. That was the festival.

Regardless of that not-so-festive festival, I do enjoy the churches here in Arezzo. Because of its crossroads situation geographically, between Florence to the north and Rome to the south, lots and lots of really, really important artists have passed through this town. Vasari was born here. Da Vinci painted an Arezzo landscape—including a still-standing bridge that we have ridden over—as the background of the *Mona Lisa*. Michelangelo was friends with Vasari and was born in Arezzo province. Many of these masters left some of their brilliant works right here in the churches. Saint Dominic's boasts an amazing Cimbue crucifix hanging over its altar. Saint Badia's has a magnificent Vasari painting. And the most famous fresco of Early Renaissance painter Piero della Francesca, *The Legend of the True Cross*, is still right smack on the walls of the little stone church in Piazza San Francesco that sits directly across from my favorite hangout, Caffé dei Costanti.

Lulu and I have been in them all. It hasn't been for their worship services, because neither my Latin nor my Italian is so good, but it has been to see the masterpieces and soak up the atmosphere. The atmosphere of Arezzo's *Santa Maria della Pieve* church is the most spine-tingling to me. It is right off of the *Piazza Grande* in the historic center of town with an ancient ornate exterior and cavernous, dark, mysterious interior lit solely by candles. Lulu was enthralled the first time we visited. I didn't even need to tell her to be quiet.

We came to one side of the nave, where the light was brighter due to the tiered stands holding dozens of prayer and offering candles. Just put your coins in the box and you can choose from tea lights, slender tapers, or red glass hurricane candles with a little picture of the Pope on the outside.

"Mama, I want to light a candle," Lulu said.

"Well, all right, I think it would be nice too," I said. I put a Euro coin in the box and selected a taper. I had no idea what the going price for the candles were, but a Euro felt like too much for a teeny tea candle and too little for the full-on Pope bedazzled one.

"Now, I will light it, and then you are supposed to say a little prayer to God," I instructed.

"What do I say exactly?" Lulu asked.

"Say something like a nice wish," I advised. And here is Lulu's official first out-loud prayer in a Catholic Church in Arezzo, Italy:

"I wish for mommy to be a lovely lady and I will be a good and lovely girl for her too...and I want a cat and a dog."

47

(While playing the "I'm Thinking of an Animal Game")

LULU: *"Is it furry?"*
ME: *"Yes."*
LULU: *I's it little?"*
ME: *Yes."*
LULU: *"Does it walk slowly?"*
ME: *"No, it* hops *really fast."*
LULU: *(Excitedly) "Ahh! Does it have cute ears?"*
ME: *(Also excitedly) "Yes!"*
LULU: *"Is it a baby kangaroo?"*
ME: *"Uhm, no."*

EIGHT

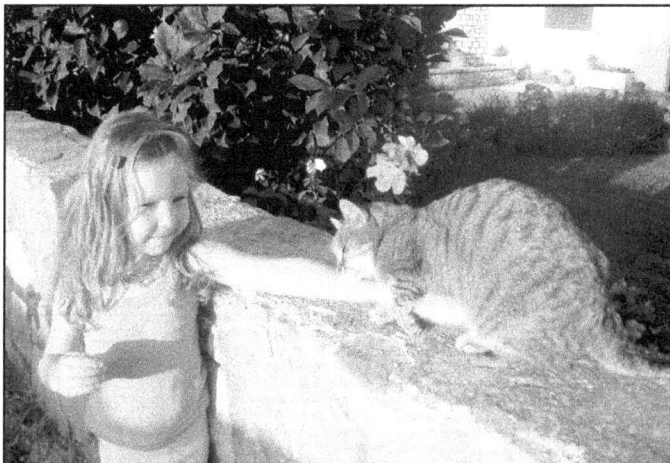

EVERY GOOD GIRL
DESERVES PETS

♦ ♦ ♦ ♦ ♦ ♦ ♦ ♦ ♦ ♦ ♦ ♦

SCORPIONS DO NOT COUNT

I HAD TWO MEMORABLE PETS growing up. Coco was a sweet-hearted Weimaraner who was deathly afraid of thunder and would cower in a closet whenever it rained. Gin was a rotund Siamese who wasn't afraid of anything. He was all purring and sweetness to us, but he was so mean to everybody else that the vet had my mom cover his face with a sock each time we took him in so he wouldn't be able to bite the doctor.

Lulu likes me to tell her stories of both them. She giggles when I describe how fierce old, portly Gin kitty was and she says, "Awww," when I tell her how I loved Coco so much that I wrote a song for my pup that I used to sing and play on the piano when I was a girl. I wrote the sheet music myself, drawing out shaky lines for the grand staff, carefully curling around the bass and treble clefs, and placing notes just so. A while back, I discovered the two pieces of paper in my mom's basement and was completely embarrassed by my then innocent lyrics:

> *"Coco bay-ee-bee,*
> *Coco dog-ee-eee*
> *Coco is a goo-ood dog,*
> *Coco is my lo-ver."*

Okay, I was only seven years old, and I obviously didn't mean it in the Biblical sense. I just loved my dog. Anyway, Lulu really wishes she had a pet and, in fact, she used to. Two weeks before she was born, Scotty, who had just finished reading a biography of Charles Schulz, said maybe we should get a beagle. Yes, you heard me: "Let's get a puppy at the same time we're about to have our first child!" We were crazy.

We drove out from our home in Denver to a farm in central Colorado and came back with the cutest baby beagle ever. He really was adorable, and of course his name had to be Snoopy. His little bed was just under Lulu's bassinet. We called them twins, except Snoopy could run and jump at three months while Lulu could not. And teeth? The inside of Lulu's mouth was as smooth as a cue ball, but Snoopy already had all of his and chewed anything he could grab. He would tear and gnaw at all of his toys and many of Lulu's, too. Lulu's teddy bear Vincent was one of the earliest of Snoopy's victims. (He was the culprit who tore off Vincent's ear, thereby inspiring the bear's name.)

Unfortunately, when Scotty was accepted into the American University in Paris, we knew we couldn't take Snoopy with us. But, we refused to put one of those ads in Craigslist or wherever that read: "Moving. Pet free to good home." Seemed so callous and uncaring. We wanted to make sure Snoopy really did go to a good home. Indeed, he got a *great* home. One of my mom's bridge friends knew a girl in grad school who lived on a farm in Indiana. She was also a professional horse woman, who jumped in shows and clearly loved animals. Betsy still posts pictures of Snoopy to me on Facebook and refers to us as his "birth parents." So, when we say that Snoopy "went to live on a farm," we really mean it and it's terrific.

But that story doesn't assuage Lulu. She wants a new pet. Now.

"I know I would like a doggie," she says with a perfectly angelic smile. "I would take care of it every day. For real."

I tell her that we just can't have a dog right now.

"We live in Italy. We can pet the dogs in our neighborhood. We're renting this house so we can't take in a dog. Antonella and Tiziano (our landlords who live next door), already have a dog you can play with." I try to reason with her with whatever I can think of. Then I try to make up for our lack of a pet by pointing out all the other really neat animals and creatures that live all around us in Tuscany besides Kika, our landlords' Maltese Terrier.

"Look, Lulu, there's a *lucerto*," I said, pointing out one of the tiny lizards that bask in the sun on the rock walls that border the homes here as we walk to school. She likes those. They're cute. I even caught and held a baby lizard one day and put it her hand. That got her thinking, though.

"There are not also scorpions and snakes on our path to school, are there, Mama?" she asked.

Maybe my pet diversion tactic hadn't been such a good one. While Tuscany is home to cute little rock lizards, it's also home to vipers and scorpions.

I grew up in a tiny rural town in Indiana actually called Farmland, which pretty much summed up the flavor of my childhood. My sister, brother, and I were country kids. Running barefoot, playing with crawdads (they may be "crayfish" to you) in the creek, and poking hornets' and bees' nests with sticks to see what would happen. We were pretty fearless.

I taught Lulu to be a "tough girl" and run barefoot, too.

"I am super brave! I am not afraid of monsters. I am not afraid of dinosaurs," she proclaimed upon our arrival in Italy. "AND I can walk barefoot on gravel."

That is better than me. I may still walk around on our patio and in the grass here in Arezzo, but walking barefoot on our gravel driveway is now out of my pain threshold. Our Italian landlords think it's all quite funny, because no one goes anywhere barefoot in Tuscany. Probably because of the vipers and the scorpions.

After we moved here, Scotty went online and did a little research about the creatures indigenous to this region (maybe we should've done that *before* we moved here). The computer warned that Tuscan vipers are poisonous and as for Lulu's question of seeing one on the path, the truth is I did see a snake on the path once. I was alone on the way to pick up Lulu, while on the phone, actually, with my mom, when one slithered out of the tall grass a couple of feet toward me. I screamed and it turned right around the way it had come. After I calmed down and remembered to tell my mom I hadn't been ambushed and killed right before her listening ears, I realized I also hadn't taken time to notice what kind of snake it may have been—poisonous or not.

The same computer entry went on to explain that while the vipers are dangerous, the scorpions found here are quite harmless, with stings no worse than those from a bee or a wasp. That didn't reassure me even though I was familiar with the stinging fliers. I know about bees and wasps. I grew up with them in Indiana. I speak their language. I have no problem capturing one under a glass, placing a card on the open side, and carrying it outside to safety. In my whole country-kid life, I've only been stung twice, once while fishing at Girl Scout camp and the other time as an adult while I was conducting a live TV news interview in Washington.

"I am not afraid of rats or mice. I am not afraid of cheetahs," Lulu has said. "I am not afraid of lions. I'm not afraid of elephants. I'm not afraid of horses. I'm not afraid of anything."

But scorpions? I didn't grow up with them. I've never lived in a place with their kind. Unlike bees and wasps, I don't speak their language. Maybe I'm an arthropod xenophobe, or maybe it has something to do with the 80's German heavy metal band, but I was afraid.

I didn't tell Lulu about my fear and Scotty was calm about it. Our new friends laughed and said it's "*Normale*! The leetle scorpions are no beeg deal and for sure you will get a scorpion in your house. *Non c'e un problema.*"

And one hot August night, it happened.

Lulu had been playing "beauty shop" with me in the living room. She'd dumped out every barrette she owned all over everywhere and put about a third of them in my hair. Now she was in bed. I'd picked up all the scattered barrettes I could find and taken my hair back down. It was about 10 p.m.

Scotty was reading in the chair and I got up for something. There, on the white tile floor in the dim lamp light near the couch where we had been playing, was a little blackish blob. I thought, "Must be another barrette."

I walked over to it, in my bare feet, of course, and reached down to pick it up. There were only about six inches between my outstretched fingers and that "barrette" before I screamed:

"EEEEE!! A scorpion!"

"What do you want me to do?" Scotty asked.

"KILL it!" I replied, without hesitation.

Scotty grabbed his boots. Then, in an instant, an icky *crunch*. I handed him a bunch of paper towels while I faced the other way and scrunched my eyes shut. I jumped up and down and squealed, "Oh my God, ohmygod, omahgaaaah! It really was a scorpion!" I felt that nervous, heart-pounding feeling you get right before you have to speak in public.

Then I felt sheepish. I mean, it was only about the size of a fifty cent piece. They're not supposed to be worse than a bee, and I never kill bees.

When I told Lulu about it the next morning she said, "I would like a garden but with bugs and scorpions who are not allowed in."

So, I'd come face to face with my indigenous creature fears, but I still hadn't sufficiently answered Lulu's question of getting a pet.

And she picked up the theme again. Cats. Now it's cats. She wants a cat.

"I love bad kitties and good kitties," she says. "All kitties. Mostly good ones though."

One of the best I've ever met happens to live right in our neighborhood. She is a wonderfully friendly tortoiseshell we call "*tartaruga*," or turtle, in honor of her coloring and her longevity. Our neighbor Massimiliano says she is around fifteen years old or so, although no one knows for sure. She is no one's cat in particular so she doesn't have a formal name, but everyone seems to know her, feed her, and love her.

We are no exception. Lulu looks for her almost every day after school and takes her a little bowl of milk when she can. Tartaruga appreciates it and purrs and rubs her head against Lulu, but she doesn't go home with anyone. She's the real-life cat from my beloved Rudyard Kipling's *Just So Stories* : "The cat walked by himself and all places were alike to him."

Our neighbors, Marzia and Nicola, have a new kitten. Her name was Mew at first, but then they changed it to Otto when they realized she was a he. Lulu now calls it, "Otto last name Mew." But she hasn't stroked it.

Maybe it's too small; Lulu won't say she's a little bit afraid of it, she just says she's not ready to touch it yet. I tell her, "There are plenty of kittens in the world. When you are ready, there will be one ready for you." That has seemed to be a good way to put off the pet-talk. Lulu has agreed she is not quite ready.

On the way to the park the other day, Lulu said she was still not ready for a "baby cat," but she was ready to sing a song about getting a kitten.

"This is about a kitten who tries to climb the rainbow," she said.

"The little cat he was so very little
and then one daaaaay,
He tried to climb...
he tried to climb...
then 'Help,' he said."

"The end," Lulu said abruptly.

"I don't think that was enough," I said, thinking that actually it was already a whole lot better than my song about my Weimaraner Coco. "I don't think you told me all that happened."

"That was just the promo," Lulu said. "I don't know the end of it yet."

So the story of Lulu and her pets, like the song, is one that will remain, for now, at least, unfinished.

♦ ♦ ♦ ♦ ♦ ♦ ♦ ♦ ♦

"Is it true, Puss-in-Boots loved womans a lot? Because womans like you are nice, Mama. That's why he loved them."

♦ ♦ ♦ ♦ ♦ ♦ ♦ ♦ ♦

NINE

IN PURSUIT OF PUMPKIN
PERFECTION

* ◆ ◆ ◆ ◆ ◆ ◆ ◆ ◆ ◆ ◆ ◆ ◆

TRICK OR TREAT BY ANY OTHER NAME
WOULD TASTE AS SWEET

I T ALL BEGAN IN PARIS with the search for the Great Pumpkin. No, we didn't sit shivering in a pumpkin patch all night like Sally and Linus. This expedition involved me combing the streets of the 15th *arrondissement* where we lived, desperately looking for a proper pumpkin to carve up for Lulu's first big Halloween.

Of course, I don't remember my first or even my second Halloween. But I remember seeing photos of me at about three years old sitting on the kitchen floor with my mom wearing her then wildly fashionable cat-eyes glasses. Newspapers are spread around and a great big pumpkin is sitting on top of them with its top cut off. We are smiling and both proudly raising our arms to my dad, who was no doubt the photographer, displaying four handfuls of the squishy, seedy, pulpy ick that was inside.

My Quixotic quest in Paris was to recreate that all-American childhood scene. I scoured almost every small grocer's stand or *supermarché* and only found some rouge squashes labeled *citrouille* (pumpkin), but which looked more like flattened turbans than what I was dreaming of. You could buy them whole, but it was *de rigueur* to purchase a smaller chunk wrapped in plastic that immediately reminded me of buying pizza by the slice.

I have since learned that they're a kind of heirloom pumpkin, but the skin is really hard and tough. They may be sought after by French gourmands to make terrific soup, but they were absolutely not suitable for carving the jack-o'-lantern visage I imagined.

So, I went back in search of the pale-orange (not red), softer-skinned and much *roundier*-faced pumpkins I grew up with in the U.S. But, like my separate (and ultimately equally in vain) Paris search for a wide selection of women's solid antiperspirants, what's ubiquitous in one country is not so in another.

We already knew that Parisians don't really do Halloween. Grown-ups might whoop it up at the bars (any excuse for a party), but there are no costumes for sale, no trick-or-treating, no bobbing for apples, really not much of nothin' for the kiddos. At Lulu's *garderie* (daycare) La Rimbambelle—which translates terrifically into "flock" and refers to a Belgian comic strip series about a group of little kids, much like the old *Our Gang* series—the wonderful teachers decided to honor their single American student and hold a costume *fête*. But they knew so little of what to do. Rodolfo, Lulu's favorite teacher, who had once trained with the famous French mime Marcel Marceau, had to even have me help him spell the holiday for the parents' memo.

"Ees eet like dees: 'A-l-o-w-i-n-e'?" he asked, spelling it in perfect phonetic French.

"Uhm, no," I said, making my laugh sound like I was clearing my throat instead. "It's a little longer, like this: 'H-a-l-l-o-w-e-e-n'."

"Eengleesh makes no sense."

And that from a French speaker.

The morning of the party, Lulu wore a green, sparkly Tinkerbell outfit that Scotty procured from the good old American Disney Store on the Champs-Elysées, since there were no other places that sold Halloween costumes. Then she proceeded to be terrified by the make-shift clown costume that Florence, La Rimbabelle's director, wore as she greeted Lulu at the school's check-in counter.

By now it was the week of Halloween and I was making larger and larger concentric circles around our apartment building, expanding my pumpkin search to neighborhoods I had never been in. I did find some of those tiny miniature pumpkins at the department/grocery store Monoprix and was becoming resigned to the idea that Lulu and I would just have to paint little faces on them. My preconceived Hallmark-moment of Daddy carving a face on a giant orange pumpkin with Lulu looking on in glee would have to wait.

Then, suddenly, I did a double-take passing a Tunisian market I had never visited before. There, in a small sidewalk display nestled among heads of cabbage, apples, and other autumn produce, were about four or five small orange (not red), roundy (not flat), regular, good old-fashioned jack-o'-lantern style pumpkins! They were even brightly labeled "Halloween Pumpkins"—in English and spelled correctly. They were a bit on the small-side—about a third of the size from the photo of my own jack-o'-lantern experience at age three—but at this point I was no position to complain.

I happily gathered my purchase in my arms like a chubby new puppy and carried it back home to our apartment. I had a long walk ahead of me and that fat puppy became increasingly heavier with every step. After the 20th block, I thanked the stars a larger pumpkin like I had imagined had not been in stock.

That night I helped Lulu scoop, Scotty carved, and we snapped a few photos. I put the candle inside the finished product and triumphantly placed it on a table underneath a window. Then I rushed us down the elevator and we looked up expectantly to our fourth floor flat. Our jack-o'-lantern was so small, you could barely distinguish its candle glow from where we stood below on the street. I felt a little less than triumphant.

Fast forward to our first Halloween in Tuscany. In the agricultural heart of Italy, big-bright-orange-roundy pumpkins are aplenty. Our equally big-hearted neighbors, Silvia and Mauro, were eager to help us have a full-out, American-style Halloween with jack-o'-lanterns, costumes, trick-or-treating, the works. Their adorable children, Alessio, who is seven and a perfect big brother figure to Lulu, and Lara, who, at three years old was about the same age as Lulu and made for a perfect "frenemy," were both excited, too.

As in Paris, children trick-or-treating house to house is not the norm in Italy either, but Mauro and Silvia invited us to dinner on Halloween night and offered to help all the kids go around hollering "*Dolcetto o Scherzetto*" (literally "Sweets or Jokes," but the lovely rhyming equivalent to "Trick or Treat!"). It sounded like a blast.

The festive events started a few days before our dinner, when Mama Silvia, as Lulu calls her, drove over to our house with her kids and delivered an assortment of pumpkins from her dad's *orto,* or vegetable garden.

"Ewww! They are still all covered in mud," Lulu squealed.

"That's just 'cause they're super fresh from the garden," I shushed.

Alessio and Lara helped carry them to our front terrace and place them on the picnic table. I put on Halloween music—think "Monster Mash" over and over—and Lulu and I brought out the Halloween snacks we made earlier in the day. "Witch's fingers," which were actually bread sticks with tips of almond slivers for creepy nails, and "mummy face" mini -pizzas with strategically placed black olives forming staring eyes and thin slices of mozzarella becoming the mummy's wrapping. We all scooped and carved away, and Alessio carefully picked out the choicest morsels from our bucket of pumpkin guts to personally oversee the baking and salting of the seeds to crispy perfection. Our carving party was the typical boisterous, all-American kid-style fun, except for the notable difference of the background terrain being dotted by Tuscan cypress and olive trees.

Finally, the big Halloween *cena,* or dinner, night arrived. Lulu wanted to be her favorite scary monster, a zombie, so I grabbed the face-paint and Scotty grabbed a bottle of wine to take over to Mauro and Silvia's. The inside of their house was streaming with orange and black decorations; they had even managed to find balloons imprinted with "Happy Halloween" in English. I thought to myself that clearly the Italians knew a thing or two more about doing Halloween for kids than the Parisians. Since we hadn't been invited over until seven o'clock, I presumed we'd go out and let the kids gather candy right away before it got too late and we'd eat dinner afterward.

I was wrong.

First, I noticed that Lara and Alessio were still in their street clothes. Maybe we weren't going to go right away. Well, soon, I imagined. Then Mama Silvia began busying herself in the kitchen preparing some *antipasti* and Mauro sauntered over to the bar to begin pouring a round of drinks. Silvia called over her shoulder that her sister and her husband were going to arrive a little later, so, "Why don't the kids go on into the living room and watch some TV and play games?" They ran off and a grown-up cocktail hour developed. The sister and her husband arrived and I looked at my watch. Eight o'clock.

Time passed. More drinks were poured. Finally, at 9:00 p.m., we sat down to dinner. Our bottle of wine was opened. Ravioli was dished out. Lulu's zombie face paint was now a smeary remnant of its former ghoulishness. She and Lara were alternately playing with, and then fighting over, a plush robot dog, which, as I kept (ridiculously) saying to them, didn't belong at the table. Alessio was finished with his dinner in two seconds and was trying on his Dracula teeth, laughing maniacally. Scotty and I were just looking at each other. Culture. Shock.

By the time my younger sister Andrea and little brother Brad were old enough to go trick-or-treating with me, we were all dressed and out the door by 5:30 p.m. at the latest. By 9:00 p.m. in our hometown in Indiana, my mom would have already had each of us three kids put our Halloween candy away in the cupboard, told us to go brush our teeth, say our prayers, and tucked us firmly into our beds.

Italian kids do not adhere to the same schedules. It's nothing to be out on a summer night in Italy for a gelato and coffee with friends at say, 11:00 p.m., and see entire families with children in tow doing the very same thing. But I thought that since trick-or-treating would involve going to other people's houses and actually ringing their bells, the late hour might pose a problem. Apparently not so. Because it wasn't until around 10:00 p.m. that Mauro contentedly sighed, pushed his seat back from the table, and exclaimed, "Okay! Let's go get some candy!"

The kids all cheered and grabbed their Halloween bags. Alessio wrapped a vampire cape around his shoulders. Mama Silvia added some red "blood" drips to either side of his mouth and quickly drew a little ghost on Lara's forhead. I touched up what was left of the smeary zombie-mess on Lulu's face. We were, uhm, off.

Now to better picture this scene, let me take a moment to explain that we live *in campagna,* which is to say, in the country, way outside our town's medieval walls. We're not in the suburbs; there are no suburbs here. You'll not find suburban-style close-clusters of identically painted houses surrounding a cul-de-sac, but rather a widespread scattering of Italian-style stuccoed and red-tiled compounds in the Tuscan countryside, each surrounded by an imposing wrought iron fence with an entrance buzzer box on the outside.

If I, or my little sister or brother had ever rung someone's doorbell at 10:00 p.m. on Halloween night, we would've been spanked by my mom, because why on earth were we outside that late? Or more likely, considering the small town in which we grew up, the offended neighbor, whose bell we had rung, would've taken a peek outside and called our mother on the phone themselves to personally advise her to spank us because...why on earth were we out that late?

I was worried about our neighbors' impending reactions now and we were soon to find out. These Italian "compound" houses, as I refer to them, are large, rambling buildings with several apartments and which often serve as multi-family dwellings. So, here at Silvia and Mauro's, all the kids had to do was run around to the side of the house, climb the stairs, and knock on their first victim's door.

The door opened and now, at about 10:20 p.m., they bellowed in unison the Italian equivalent to "Trick or Treat": "*Dolcetto o Scherzetto!*"

Lulu had been practicing this rhyming tongue twister for days and at that moment, along with Lara and Alessio, she got it right in intent, if not in perfect Italian diction. Smiling, Cousin Francesca, still somehow stylishly dressed and fresh-looking at this time of night, welcomed them in. It didn't appear at all that she would urge any spankings; in fact, she seemed delighted to see them. They chattered in Italian and then she dropped something that looked like a huge brick, from my vantage point, into each of the kids' bags. Not a mini-Snickers, or a tiny Reese's cup, mind you, this turned out to be a five-inch long chunk of chocolate fondant. The kids tore out from there and ran screaming downstairs to Silvia's aunt and uncle's apartment.

"*Dolcetto o scherzetto!*"

Here they were again happily greeted and each received a *Kinder Sorpresa*. Lulu loves them. They're remarkable hollow chocolate eggs encasing a tiny plastic toy or figurine inside. You'll be hard-pressed to find them in the U.S. because, of course, the toy poses way too much of a choking hazard. They're like a Cracker Jack back when Cracker Jack toys were cool and not just some lame paper puzzle.

It's now around 11:00 p.m. The kids run shrieking out of the family compound into the narrow street to the closest neighbor's house. Surely for an actual unrelated neighbor, this hour is too late, I think. Alessio rings the buzzer, and I am surprised as the gate immediately clicks open. The kids continue bellowing up the stairs to the door of Mara and Roberto's—an older couple who speak not a word of English, but to whom I have politely saluted with a cheery "*Buongiorno*" every time I've seen them. I hope that gesture perhaps softens the blow we are sure to receive.

"*Dolcetto o scherzetto!*" the kids cry out again.

Inexplicably, this door opens, too, and as the children go in, I strain to hear. It's too muffled to make out anything. But after a few moments, the children emerge victorious, not spanked, again!

Finally, my favorite moment of the evening arrives as now the terrorizing trio stride purposefully across the street to Marzia and Nicola's house. They're a young couple with an adorable, chubby little toddler, Francesco, or Franci, for short. They're always friendly when we pass by, but I think that with such a young one, they must be finished for the evening by now. Obviously, not sharing or concerned by any of my thoughts, Alessio leads the way for the kids and rings the gate's buzzer.

Nothing happens, and instead of playing it safe, Mauro calls out to them and suggests they assemble underneath the first floor window that faces onto the street. The shutter is, of course, closed. But undaunted, Mauro actually raps his fist on the window.

"No way! I can't even believe this," I whisper to Scotty.

In only a few seconds, the shutters open. Marzia leans down holding onto a not-looking-sleepy-at-all baby Franci. I have never seen either parent without a cigarette, and even now, she first puts out her cigarette in the empty flower box on the windowsill and then smiles down at the kids.

"*Dolcetto o scherzetto!*" rings out again.

And at 11:15 p.m., a variety of goodies soon came tumbling down from that window into the bags being held up by six outstretched little arms. Turns out the goodies were some sort of bittersweet squares of cooking chocolate. But, for *waaay* past 5:30 p.m. and for a holiday Italians don't officially even celebrate, it was a very successful night for two local children and a certain American three-year-old.

I, however, was exhausted.

◆ ◆ ◆ ◆ ◆ ◆ ◆ ◆ ◆

"I love you and if you want some of my pizza, you can have the crust, because I do not like the crust."

◆ ◆ ◆ ◆ ◆ ◆ ◆ ◆ ◆

TEN

DO YOU BELIEVE IN MAGIC?

MY MAGIC WAND'S NOT WORKIN'!

L ULU WAS WEARING LIGHT BLUE fairy wings, a plastic "jewel"-studded crown, and carrying a silver wand tipped with a sparkly star. She was running around the living room pointing it at everything. She was mysteriously chanting part of an incantation she heard *Strega* (witch) Luana say on the long-running Italian children's TV show, *Melavisione*, as she waved it.

"*Magia, magia…*" she intoned, aiming the wand at the couch. "Turn into a pony!"

The couch stayed a couch.

Then, the other morning while Scotty was still sleeping, I asked Lulu to please go and tell him the coffee was ready. Lulu first went to her room to retrieve her wand. I saw her emerge armed and ready and then head over toward our room. I couldn't see her, but I heard her open our door. I imagined her standing next to the bed passing the wand over Scotty's recumbent body as I heard her call out in a low voice, "*Magia, magia*...Daddy, wake up!"

There was a pause. I figured Scotty, who had undoubtedly heard Lulu's spell, had also chosen not to open his eyes. And then I heard, in a voice full of real surprise and disappointment: "Heeey! My magic wand's not workin'!"

Lulu wasn't astounded by her wand malfunctions simply because, like so many preschoolers, she's at that point in her life where everything is possible. She was surprised her wand didn't work because she really, truly, *extremely* believes in magic having been surrounded by it since birth. Lulu has witnessed billiard balls multiply and fresh eggs appear— seemingly from nowhere. She has been on-hand as ropes were cut and then restored. She has looked on as beautiful ladies were sawed in half. At only four, she's seen it all.

Because Lulu's daddy happens to be a magician. Not like your crazy uncle with that old deck of TV Magic Cards, Lulu's daddy is an honest-to-God professional who has performed around the world in clubs and cabarets, notable and notorious. Scotty went to his first magic show when he was just eight and has been studying and performing magic ever since. His shows have included everything from sleight-of-hand card tricks, Houdini-style water escapes, to a sophisticated retro "Devil's Bar Act" wherein he conjures a variety of classic cocktails and distributes them to audience members to verify—and enjoy.

Lulu hasn't taken part in the spirited spirits act quite yet, but she has been "assisting" her dad since before she could form full sentences. When she was about two, for instance, she would giggle in wonder as Scotty made coins apparate from behind her ears.

We lived in Paris then, and one day Lulu and I went to the Post Office in our *quartier*, or neighborhood. The branch's manager, Didier, spoke a little English so whenever he saw us, he liked to come by and chat with me and pat Lulu on the head. This day he was eager to show us their newly installed automated stamp machines (all the post offices in Paris have them now, and they're a much needed improvement over waiting forever in a long queue just to buy a single postcard stamp from a cranky clerk). With Didier's guidance, we quickly and easily bought our stamps. Then the machine spat out our change in a little metal cup.

The change cup was exactly in reach of Lulu from where she sat below in her *pousette* (stroller). Before you could say "choking hazard," she grabbed a coin. Then she looked up at us, raised said coin, put it behind her own ear, and then brandished it out again with a flourish that would've made Siegfried and Roy proud.

Didier looked at me, not sure of what he had just seen.

"I think she just performed a magic trick for you," I explained, not exactly sure what I had witnessed myself.

"But shee eez no more than two," Didier gasped.

"I know, but her father is a magician."

"*C'est vrais?* That eez eencredible. I must see it again."

And with that, he bent his head down to her level and pointed to his ear. She lifted the coin and put it behind his ear for a second, then swept her hand out in a flutter of reappearance. Obviously, she didn't get the part about how you're not supposed to let your audience see the coin *before* you produce it, but she had the general idea. Didier was nearly brought to tears of laughter.

Here in Tuscany, in between Scotty's academic studies, he has performed his cabaret act numerous times in private villas, on stage, and in the Piazza del Duomo. Lulu and I almost always go. Befitting a classic magician, Scotty wears a sartorial tuxedo with tails. And now, our daughter, who is much older than when she first began "performing" in Paris, but not any wiser at knowing how tricks are done, demands to be dressed just as smartly.

"Not old play clothes, Mama, I want something lovelier," she said one evening. I tossed aside the sooty rags I was going to put her in, and picked out a cute-as-a-button black wool crepe dress. "I have to look lovely, because I'm Daddy's 'assist,'" Lulu said.

She has been chosen as one of his volunteer assistants so many times that last week, when we passed a big billboard in town promoting Scotty's latest cabaret, *Hollywood Arezzo*, Lulu looked up at the black and white photo of her dad on the sign and studied it for a while. Then she turned and asked me, "Why isn't my picture up there? I'm Daddy's helper."

There was one time when Scotty didn't select Lulu. The crowd was full of kids and he didn't want it to seem unfair to the others by picking his daughter. When Lulu realized the show was over and she hadn't had a chance to come up and help, she cried and cried. Now, if she's in the room, it's standard practice to have her come on stage to assist in Scotty's opening trick, "The Multiplying Bunnies."

The hall is dark and the spotlight shines on Lulu's dad.

"I'd like to start with a little trick with some bunnies," Scotty calls out. "Anybody out there in the audience who likes bunnies? Everyone say, 'Yes!'"

Voices ring out, "Yes!" And hands from random kids – and, of course, from Lulu – shoot up in the air.

Scotty points over to her in the front row. (She always sits in the front row.)

"Would you like to help me? Come on up here. Come on up."

Lulu steps up to the stage and it's like they have never met.

"What's your name?" Scotty asks.

Not acting, she is shy and bashful, holding her hands in front of her and rocking a bit from side to side. She never has said, "Daa-aad, you know my name." She always softly replies, "Lulu."

"Everyone say, 'Hiii, Lulu!'" Scotty says, encouraging the audience.

The crowd choruses back with a big, "Hiii Lulu!" Lulu smiles and gives a little sheepish smile toward the audience.

"Wait 'til you see what happens, Lulu!" Scotty continues in his big show voice. "Here are my bunnies," he says, holding two egg-sized, red, bunny-shaped sponges. "Aren't they cute?"

She gently nods and starts to reach her hand out. Scotty pulls his hand back and displays the bunnies to the audience. "Aren't they cute? Wait 'til you see what they do."

Now he lifts his foot and places one of the sponge bunnies on the toe of his shoe. "I'm going to put Mama Bunny right here on my shoe. Right there, so everyone can see her. Right there."

Then he extends his left hand and says, "And here's Papa Bunny right here. I'll keep Papa and I'm going to give you Mama Bunny, here." He shuts his hand around Papa Bunny. Then he lifts Mama Bunny from his foot and places her inside Lulu's hand, closing her fingers around it. "Hold Mama Bunny right there. Very tight."

He then lifts her closed hand up over her head. "Hold your hand up high so everyone can see! Good! Now we're going to say the magic words. The magic words go like this, 'Papa, go to Mama!'"

Scotty yells the words down at his own closed fist as if he is urging Papa to somehow jump over into Lulu's little hand. Lulu is standing next to him with her fist over her head.

"Papa, go to Mama," Lulu repeats the magic words. She doesn't need to be prompted like some other kids to say the words aloud. She knows her part. She is still standing next to her dad with her fist over her head.

"That's great! She's doin' it!" Scotty exclaims.

They say the magic words again together a couple of times. "Papa, go to Mama!" Lulu is still standing next to him with her fist over her head, but her arm is beginning to sag. Scotty then blows on his closed fist and opens his hand with a flourish showing that Papa Bunny is not there. Scotty's hand is empty. "Look," he says. "He went!"

Scotty turns to Lulu. "Open your hand," he says to her. She is now smiling broadly and opens her hand showing the two bunnies have mysteriously come together in her little palm. The crowd gives a collective "Ahhh!"

Scotty asks, "How did you do that?!"

Lulu's eyes are always wide. No answer.

"Don't tell me, I don't want to know," Scotty says. Laughter comes from the crowd.

"That was the easy part," Scotty goes on. "Now, we're going to show them the hard part. Are you ready?" He looks down at Lulu and she is full of anticipation. She looks back up at him and says, "Mmm-hmm!"

"I'm going to give you both bunnies," Scotty says. "Papa and Mama. Hold them both really tight. That's a lot of responsibility. Are you excited?" He places a red blob of sponge in her hand and again folds it up over her head.

"Okay, squeeze them tight. We're going to say the magic words. The magic words are like this, 'Bunnies go back.'" He claps his hands for effect.

"Bunnies go back," Lulu says.

Scotty starts shaking his right arm in an apparent effort to get the bunnies to reappear in his closed right hand. He shimmies and shakes his arm. It looks like he's trying to convince those little red sponge bunnies to slide down his tuxedo sleeve into his fist.

Lulu is still standing next to her dad with her fist over her head. The crowd begins to giggle. Scotty shakes his arm again. "This is the reason I make the big bucks, because of this part right here," he says. "It's true. I sometimes make up to four Euros an hour doing this on the Corso."

Now he's pulling at his cuff and looking up the sleeve. "It's tough," he says. "I'm wearing a different shirt tonight. I was rushed." He wipes his brow while Lulu remains standing. Her little arm is starting to get heavy again and begin to sink lower. After what seems like a long time, he finally turns to her and says, "You're holding 'em so tight, you're gonna kill 'em, Lulu!" He pulls her closed hand down to him and opens it.

The crowd gasps, "Ohhhhhhh!!" as Mama, Papa, *and* a surprising shower of little sponge baby bunnies come cascading out of Lulu's hand onto the stage.

"Oh! That is not what I expected to happen," her dad, the magician, says. "But aren't those the cutest bunnies you've ever seen?"

The crowd is laughing and clapping while Lulu puts her index finger in her mouth in astonishment. "Give her a round of applause!" Scotty shouts.

They do and she is radiant. She knows what's going to happen in the trick because she has been doing it all her life. All four years. But, of course, she doesn't know *how* it happened. Her daddy didn't even use a magic wand. He just uses words. Lulu seemed to have latched on to that nuance as she recently confided to me she now knows her wand is "just pretend."

"But," she added, "I need the right words. That makes the magic."

Scotty says there are mainly two types of people who go to magic shows. The combative types who scrutinize every move, determined to beat the magician and "figure out" each trick. And the type of spectator who comes simply to be entertained. To suspend disbelief and enjoy the wonder of the art.

I hope Lulu stays in the latter category.

◆　◆　◆　◆　◆　◆　◆　◆　◆

(In a conversation with Daddy)

DADDY: *"When I was in school I
got all A's."*
LULU: *"Where?"*
DADDY: *"Where what??"*
LULU: *"I mean, where are they
now? Where did you put
them??!"*

◆　◆　◆　◆　◆　◆　◆　◆　◆

ELEVEN

TESTING GRAVITY

$\bullet \quad \bullet \quad \bullet \quad \bullet \quad \bullet \quad \bullet \quad \bullet \quad \bullet \quad \bullet \quad \bullet \quad \bullet \quad \bullet$

A HELLO KITTY BAND-AID CAN'T
FIX EVERYTHING

M Y EARLIEST HUMAN MEMORY is naturally a vague one. I am three years old, sitting on the stoop of the first house my family lived in at 101 Sutherland Street in LaPorte, Indiana. I can see myself playing with some decorative stones or pea gravel that must've been scattered around our stoop. Another little girl is there and she apparently wants the pebbles I have in my hand pretty badly, because, in the next blurry image I have, I see her grabbing my hand and biting my wrist.

That's it. I don't know who the little girl was or if my mom put a Band-Aid on my arm or what. Mom said the way I described the front stairs with the pea gravel is right on, and there were lots of other little girls living on our block back then, so who knows?

In our neighborhood here in Arezzo, Lulu's darling little friend, Lara, bit her the other day. They were playing over at Lara's house, so I didn't witness the attack. But when I came to pick Lulu up after their playdate, she was sporting a Band-Aid on her right arm. Mama Silvia explained that Lulu wouldn't hand over some toy that Lara asked for and so Lara impulsively bit her. Sounded familiar. But Lara didn't bite hard; there wasn't even a mark. And I wouldn't have expected there would be because Lara is really one of the most tender-hearted kids I know. Not a known piranha. But, of course, it was no matter. Get an owie, get a Band-Aid—that's the rule.

I suppose I shouldn't keep calling them Band-Aids, since the strips Mama Silvia used here in Italy were not "The Official #1 Adhesive Bandage in America" (as the Band-Aid website proclaims). But this Italian brand had certainly caught on to America's #1 tradition of targeted marketing, as its bandages were emblazoned with cartoon characters designed to turn children into little monsters who loudly demand to be bandaged each and every time they get a scrape, cut, or a nick, no matter how minor.

Lulu didn't want to take off the Band-Aid (I am going to unapologetically use this as a generic term from now on) over the weekend, even after it was getting a little grimy around the edges. "Because it's Hello Kitty," she explained. "I will absolutely only wear Hello Kitty Band -Aids from now on."

And then on Monday when I came to take her home from school, I saw that Hello Kitty had disappeared from her arm and Ariel the Disney mermaid was now on her left knee. "I fell," Lulu proudly announced, clearly happy that her Band-Aid reign was continuing. "I will absolutely only wear Ariel Band-Aids from now on."

So during this preschooler time of climbing rope ladders at a park, balancing on the rock wall that parallels the walk up to our medieval town's ancient *Porta Stufi*, and even the occasional arm nibble, we have a variety of colorfully themed Band-Aids on hand to suit every "need." Lulu even uses them on her stuffed animals.

"Vincent has to have a Band-Aid, he hurt his ear," she said.

"That ear was bit off by Snoopy a long time ago," I countered.

"He still needs a Band-Aid." Lulu said definitively. "A Tweety Bird one."

Stuffies aside, when she balances on the rock wall or climbs the rope ladder, I know that Lulu, like almost every preschooler I suppose, is in that time of her life. She is growing, learning, and exploring. She is busy testing the boundaries of her physical limitations. What really scares me, though, is that she is also conducting tests on things about which we already definitively know the properties and their limitations. Like gravity.

"Lulu, stop rocking back on that chair," I said one day. "You're going to fall and hit your head."

"And then you'll hold me," she calmly replied.

Other accidents perplex Lulu because she knows they can't be fixed by a Band-Aid, regardless of what character is on them. Eating her cereal one morning, she suddenly screamed, "Owww!"

I looked over at her. She was still on her chair, her bowl was still in its place, and she didn't appear to be bleeding anywhere.

"What happened?"

"I bit my tongue," Lulu said. "Not a little bit. A lot. How do you not bite your tongue all the time when it lives in your mouth?"

And last summer, when we were visiting a friend's villa in the nearby Tuscan town of Cortona, Lulu was splashing around in the pool when she began yelping in pain and thrashing her left hand about. I knew it couldn't be a shark, but I couldn't imagine what might be the cause until I examined her hand closely. Her index finger was a bit swollen and a little black dot was in the middle.

"I think you got stung by your first bee," I said.

"I need a Band-Aid!" Lulu wailed.

"No, I think we need to remove the stinger and put some ice on your finger," I said.

"And then a Band-Aid."

"Okay, and then a Band-Aid," I agreed.

When I was five and in kindergarten, Woodsy Owl, that avian icon from the late 70's through the early 80's who said, "Give a hoot – don't pollute," came to our school to teach us not to litter. I evidently took his words immediately to heart. That afternoon, while I walked with my best friends Kerry and Cindy the short couple of blocks back to our homes, I gathered up all the bits of paper and trash I could find, intending to put them in a proper receptacle. This was small-town Indiana; we didn't live in a tough urban neighborhood with dangerous debris. But my haul included a broken Coke bottle that I saw lying on the curb and loaded precariously into my arms. My grasp of everything was wobbly and tenuous. I tripped on a cracked piece of sidewalk and fell down with a crash. The broken bottle sliced into my left thumb. Badly.

"Was there a lot of *sangue* (blood)?" Lulu asks every time when I tell her this story, which is one of her favorites from the "tell me a story about when you were little" anthology.

"Oh, yes," I always reply in a ghoulish voice. "There was *a lot* of blood."

In fact, there really was. It was more than any cartoon character Band-Aid would've been able to handle even if we would've had them back then. Which we didn't. There was a trail of blood that leaked from my then bright red thumb onto the pavement as Kerry, Cindy, and I ran the rest of the way to my house. We opened the gate and went straight to the front door and began to pound on it—smearing it in crimson as we did so.

"Go around to the back!" my mom called from inside. You see, our front door opened immediately to the living room which was decorated as nicely as my parents could afford on my dad's small salary working as a pilot for Borg Warner, a car parts supplier company. Mom's rule was that we were supposed to go in through the back door to the kitchen because the living room was off-limits to kids.

We knocked again a little more desperately this time, but Mom was having none of it. She, of course, had no idea what carnage awaited her. "Go. Ah-round!" she yelled again.

We ran dutifully around to the back door and my mom met us there, initially intending to chew me out for banging on the front door when I knew better, but instead, she dropped open her mouth and turned white from seeing all the red. She brought me inside and flung my hand, which, by this time really was quite covered in blood, under the faucet. She turned it on full-blast to clean off the blood to get a better look at what was going on. The force of the water almost swept away all the skin from my thumb's first joint, which was sliced through to the knuckle.

Mom did not do so well with this.

She screamed and wrapped my hand in a towel. By now, blood was everywhere. On the sink, on the kitchen counter, dripping on the floor, and of course on the back door *and* the off-limits front door. She took my little sister Andrea, who was just about two at this point, and baby Brad, who was only some months old, over to Cindy's house to be babysat by the family's eldest daughter, Kim. Mom popped me into the car and drove straight-away to the doctor's. She didn't take a moment to write an explanatory note for my dad who was still at work. And this was long before cell phones. I can only imagine what he must've thought when he arrived home to an empty house covered in blood.

There was some mention that I might lose that first joint of my thumb, but in the end, I came home with fifteen stitches and a good story.

When I think of all the adventures my brother, sister, and I went on to have, which resulted in more stitches and even a few broken bones, I marvel that any of us ever made it to adulthood. And although so far there have been no fractures or stitches, whether it's a sting, a scrape, or a bruise, Lulu comes home with some kind of mishap memento almost every week. Sometimes, when I'm getting her changed into her pajamas at night, I'll notice a little mark I haven't seen the day before.

"Where'd you get that?" I'll ask.

"I dunno," Lulu will usually say. "But I think I need a Band-Aid."

"No, you don't, get in bed," I'll answer.

It's a rite of passage and I just pray she passes through it like my sister, brother, and I did. Which was just fine—even without Hello Kitty or Ariel or whoever Band-Aids.

◆ ◆ ◆ ◆ ◆ ◆ ◆ ◆ ◆

"Don't button my pants so tight, my belly
button is going to fly out."

◆ ◆ ◆ ◆ ◆ ◆ ◆ ◆ ◆

TWELVE

THE ITALIAN GRANDPAS

· · · · · · · · · · · · ·

LULU, VICE PRESIDENT, CLOM CLUB

THE ELDERLY GENTLEMAN WHO waved at us was straight out of Central Casting for his role as "Italian Old Man." He was wearing brown pants and a short-sleeved, pale blue button-down shirt. On his sun-tanned and weathered bald head was a brimmed hat to ward off the scorching Tuscan sun, and he was leaning on a wooden cane that appeared to be hand-carved. He smiled at us as we walked toward him along the vine-yard-lined country road and brightly called out, *"Ciao, buongiorno!"*

Lulu and I waved back and answered in kind.

"Was he a CLOM?" Lulu asked after we passed.

"Yes," I answered. "I am sure he was a CLOM."

"I knew it. He looked very nice and cute," Lulu said.

My sister Andrea and I are the founders of the exclusive CLOM club. It's an international group in which none of its members ever know they've been discriminately selected. That's because we alone comprise the induction committee. Whenever Andrea or I meet, or even merely happen to view from a distance, a kindly-looking, wizened, male senior citizen, preferably of smaller stature, we internally decide whether or not he makes the cut.

Additional requirements generally include twinkling eyes—color not important. They may have some hair, but it should be at best wispy, no full fluffy heads of hair or cheesy comb-overs allowed. Most of all, they must be of a cheery disposition. No grouches, curmudgeons, or perverts. That last category has made for a few interesting club-member expulsions.

For example, after Andrea graduated from college, she back-packed around Europe with a friend. They struck up a conversation with an initially charming elderly German gentleman at some beer garden in Bavaria. I think he was wearing *lederhosen*. (No, actually I just made that up, because the image was too irresistible.) Anyway, he was apparently congenial and funny, and he generously offered to buy them a couple of steins. Andrea decided he was a prime candidate for the club, and was preparing to register him into our mental directory, when he suddenly and unexpectedly leaned way too close across the wooden *biergarten* table toward my sister. Looking longingly at her, he invited her to come privately with him to "see his wine collection."

Out. Out. Even before he was formally admitted, this guy was kicked out of the club.

And just this afternoon, literally while I was typing this exact essay on my laptop at my Arezzo version of *Cheers*, where everybody knows my name, Caffé dei Costanti, an elderly gent wearing a silk scarf with Pope John Paul II on it (for real—this time I'm not making up the picturesque attire), passed my table and looked my way.

"*Buongiorno,*" I said politely.

He stopped walking. Turned and faced me.

"Do I know you?" he asked in Italian.

"No, I'm sorry, you don't know me. I was only trying to be polite," I replied in my really bad, haltingly slow, Tarzan kind of Italian. I know I didn't use the formal "you" form. I can never remember how to do that. And I also didn't remember that the word for *polite* in Italian is *educato*. I used *pulito* instead, which actually means uhm, *clean*. Now he was laughing and asked if he could sit next to me.

"*Posso?*" he asked, meaning "May I?", as he indicated the chair across from me.

I figured he looked harmless enough, and it was lunchtime, not happy hour. So I nodded "yes."

"You are obviously not Italian. Are you British?" he asked, as he pulled up a chair.

"*No, io sono americana.*"

"Ah," he brightened. "An American girl. *Bravissima.* You are also very beautiful. Are you married?"

Oh boy. "Yes," I said hesitantly, not because of my bad Italian this time, but due to the direction this conversation appeared to be heading. "I am very married."

"Ahhh. But do you love him?"

Okay, this is not going the way I expected. Not that I knew what I expected exactly. Maybe some idle chat about how I like life in Italy, how he was in town for Pope Benedict's Mass this weekend, anything. Just something different than the wrong turn this was starting to take.

"Yes, I love him very much," I said, maybe a little too forcefully. "*Senti!* (Listen!) How old are you?" I added.

"*Settanta,*" he proclaimed proudly as he theatrically readjusted his Pope scarf.

"Seventy," I said. "Like my mom."

"Ah. Don't offend me," he said.

"Don't offend my mom," I shot back.

"Well then," he said, still smiling, "since I cannot make love to you, I will sing to you instead."

And then, incredibly, this old man sitting across from me in that ridiculous scarf suddenly burst into an Italian ballad at full operatic volume. I will admit he had a smooth voice, but I was not swept off my feet. Instead, Pietro, Caffé dei Costanti's always impeccably dressed owner, came dashing around the corner to my table and asked if everything was okay. I'm pretty sure he knew the answer was, "No," way before I opened my eyes wide and mouthed, "*Aiuto!*" (Help me!)

Fortunately, the crazy crooner noticed Pietro. He left without even paying for his coffee, which I gladly would've bought to have him depart. Okay, so that guy, too, definitely did not have what it takes to be initiated into our CLOM club.

That's because, as even little Lulu knows, the acronym CLOM stands for: Cute Little Old Men, *not* Creepy Leering Old Men.

Now the club's induction responsibilities have extended to my daughter. I have explained the name's meaning and the club's criteria to Lulu, and we enjoy finding potential new inductees as we walk the Tuscan country roads and explore Arezzo's cobbled city streets together. I also tell Lulu about the CLOM club's charter and model member, my mom's dad. The best grandpa in the universe.

Robert Gail Raven had sparkly pale blue eyes that perfectly matched the star sapphire ring he always wore on his right hand. I used to sit on his lap and peer into the ring as he moved his finger just so, until it caught the sun's rays that kindled the "star" inside the stone to dazzle brilliantly. Grampa Raven, as we called him, smiled and laughed more than easily. Not college-educated, he read voraciously and never threw away a *National Geographic* magazine. He was friendly and funny and kind to everyone. He's who I picture whenever I hear the description of someone who "never met a stranger."

A real nature lover, he took joy in hiking with his three grandkids (Andrea, me, and our little brother Brad) in the Indiana forest preserve behind his and Grannie's house. He taught us how to find delicious morel mushrooms, pick wild mulberries, and how to make tea from the root of a sassafras sapling. Every summer, our family would load up Grannie and Grampa's camper for a two week trek "Out West." I remember thrilling at seeing Yellowstone, the Grand Canyon, Mesa Verde, and the Petrified Forest, where Mom and Dad bought a stone slice of tree with gold numbers glued on it that served as our living room clock for years.

As the oldest, I got to sit in the front seat of the camper, KOA guidebook in my hands, and pick the campground where we would stay each night. If at all possible, it had to be one with a game room and a swimming pool. Grampa Raven taught me to swim and dive in one of those pools. He also taught me how to quietly appreciate the outdoors. One evening after our picnic table dinner somewhere in Arizona, he and I walked far past the rows of motor homes to stare across the empty desert at the pink sky's setting sun, interrupted here and there by a silhouette of a giant saguaro cactus.

"Listen," Grampa whispered to me.

I stood silently for a moment, my ears straining to pick up a sound. Finally, I admitted, "Grampa, I don't hear anything."

"Exactly," he replied. "Enjoy it for a while."

Grampa Raven never made it to Europe, but his namesakes both have. Andrea's six-year-old daughter Sophia's middle name is Gail, same as Grampa's was, and Lulu's middle name is his surname Raven. Every morning, along our daily walk to Lulu's preschool, I look out across the hills and fields and think of him. There are no sassafras trees here, but I try to help Lulu relish the nature we see. I point out olive and fig trees instead. We collect wildflowers and keep our eyes peeled for the occasional tiny lizard or *lucerto* that may be soaking up the sun on the low stone walls encircling our neighbors' housing compounds.

I call them "compounds" because they serve as homes for many members of extended families. Aunts, uncles, cousins, and especially the *nonni*, or grandparents, all live under one sprawling roof with several entrances making for private apartments. In the early morning, when I'm pushing Lulu's *passeggino* along the narrow roads to her school, the working-age neighbors are getting ready to leave for their jobs, or drive their kids to school, leaving the retired *nonni* free to lean out their windows and wave to us. In honor of Grampa Raven, I always wave back and then holler a friendly "*Buongiorno.*" I encourage Lulu to do the same.

"Lulu, it always makes a person smile when a little child politely greets them," I tell her.

Lulu obliges with a pipsqueak voiced version of "Ciao!" and is met with delighted reactions.

"Mama," she says, "you're right, everyone is happier now. Because of me."

In our rural neighborhood, where everyone *else* has a car, our daily strolls to and from school in rain, shine, or snow, have taken us from initial curiosity to resident fixture. Now, many of our gracious neighbors have moved from their window positions to venture outside their compound gates to talk with us face to face. They lean down and pat Lulu's head or lightly pinch her cheeks. As best I can, I try to carry on conversations about whether it will rain, how they're doing, or what's for dinner.

We've befriended quite a few *nonne,* or grandmas. Antonia is a spirited *nonna* with short, spikey, silver hair, who can often be seen cruising on her Vespa. There's also a still dark-haired Gina who loves that my name is the same as hers, even though that's unfortunately as far as my Italian heritage goes.

But it's the *nonni,* or grandpas, who really bowl me over with their generosity. For example, Palmiro only has a few remaining teeth and is pushed everywhere in a wheelchair by his nurse. But he still has a mischievous gleam in his watery blue eyes and teases Lulu, pretending to snatch her teddy bear Vincent away from her for a ride in his chair. One morning, as we were walking by his house toward Lulu's school, his nurse pushed him quickly up to his front gate and he called out, "*Ti piace...*" then something that sounded like "*oooova?*" I only understood the "*Ti piace,*" or "do you like," portion of his Italian question, but I couldn't make out the slurry word at the end—partly because my Italian wasn't so good and partly because Palmiro didn't have his dentures in.

His nurse prompted, "*Uova.*"

"Oo-oh-vaa." Oh, got it, I thought. "Eggs." That's a little strange, I then thought. But, out loud, I replied back in Italian, "Uhm, yes, we like eggs." Palmiro then smiled excitedly and said something else that sounded very slurred, which I didn't catch. I sort of just smiled and mumbled, "*Va bene, ciao!* (Okay, bye!)" and pushed Lulu along on our way.

As we continued to school, Lulu asked, "Where's his teeth, Mama? Is it true all grownups can take them out?"

"No, Lulu, and that is why you have to be sure to really brush your teeth well every night."

"Is he still a CLOM without teeth?"

"Yes, as long as he's kind, he can still certainly be a CLOM."

That afternoon, on the way home, Palmiro was sitting in his wheelchair at his gate again, waiting for us to walk by his house. I wondered if I would figure out the mystery of what he was trying to tell me earlier in the day. We approached and saw that he had an old cardboard gelato container in his lap. He held it out to me. I opened the box and saw six brown, speckled chicken eggs.

"*Fresche*," Palmiro said. Fresh. I was touched. Yes, Palmiro was indeed a CLOM.

Behind almost every house-compound in our neighborhood stands a little shed or lean-to. I wouldn't go so far as to call them proper chicken coops. We didn't know what was inside them for sure, but we had a pretty good clue from the early morning sounds of *"chi-cchir-ichi"* (Italian roosters do not say "cockle-doodle-doo*"*) that chickens were the likely possibility. And now we had a half-dozen fresh eggs from some of those very same birds. Plus, we solved the mystery of what Palmiro had told us, presuming that what he said was something along the lines of, "Come back this afternoon and I'll give you some eggs." Maybe he had said, "Wait right there, I'll be right back with some eggs." Yet we strolled along unknowingly. I'll never know. But at least it worked out.

My personal Italian CLOM favorite in our neighborhood is Rivaldo. He has smiled and waved to us from the first day we walked past. He always comes out of his house to greet us and seems genuinely interested in our lives here. He listens patiently as I try to converse in Italian. He even stopped his car and offered to drive Scotty home when he saw him trudging back from the hardware store one hot summer day. Now that Rivaldo is retired, his full-time job seems to be feeding the numerous feral cats that wander our country fields. Lulu and I see him on our walks brandishing a large can of food like the Pied Piper, only with mewing cats instead of rats circling around him. Instead of a chicken coop in his backyard, he has wooden bee hives from which he has given us two jars of the lightest, sweetest tasting Acacia honey. He more than twinkles; he practically shines.

It's not that CLOMs have to give gifts to earn entry into the club, mind you. They only have to have their hearts in the right place like the original CLOM, Grampa Raven.

So, Lulu and I have instated plenty of other Tuscan CLOMs, such as Luciano, who must be at least seventy, yet is out tending to his immaculate vegetable garden every day—even in winter. Massimo, the cherubic owner of Café Stefano along the Corso Italia in Arezzo's *centro storico,* who always greets us with a smile. Renaldo, the white-bearded man who runs the *edicola*, or newspaper stand, and recites Italian poetry while Lulu gets a *likka likka* (lollipop) and I get an *International Herald Tribune*. Even our landlord, Tiziano, has almost reached CLOM status with his silver hair and sparkly eyes. He and his wife Antonella have helped us out so much, fixing things, lending us pots to plant flowers in, bestowing presents for Lulu during holidays. But at only a little over sixty, Tiziano is still too robust.

You just can't be overly hale and hearty and make it into the CLOM club. It's good to be a little long in the tooth. Frail, but still with a spring in your step.

Or, as Lulu put it one day, after an especially nice exchange with Rivaldo: "I love all these Grandpas," she said looking up at me from her *passeggino* as we continued on our walk. "They have such nice, cutie, smiley faces. It's good to be nice to them. 'Cause they're all gonna die."

I couldn't believe my ears. But Lulu's innocently brutal statement rang true. So, to future members of the CLOM Club: Hurry. This is a special, limited-time offer.

83

♦ ♦ ♦ ♦ ♦ ♦ ♦ ♦ ♦

*(In regard to her blue, horse-shaped, helium-filled
balloon when it was decidedly thinner and lower
the next morning)*

"Aww, I'm gonna miss him when he dies."

♦ ♦ ♦ ♦ ♦ ♦ ♦ ♦ ♦

THIRTEEN

PRIVATE LULU

• • • • • • • • • • • •

PARTS OF THIS CHAPTER ARE RATED "PG,"
WHICH STANDS FOR "POOR GINA"

WE WERE STANDING NEAR the fountain at Arezzo's *Piazza Grande*, or the Grand Plaza. The weather was sunny and warm, and a lot of people were hanging around enjoying the day. There were tourists taking pictures, families eating lunch at one of the cafes lining the plaza, and there was a woman sitting on the stone steps nearby nursing an infant.

"Mama, is it true…?"

Lulu begins her more interesting observations with this introduction. I braced myself. She then very noticeably pointed over to the woman on the steps.

"Is it true that that baby's drinkin' milk from that lady's boobie?"

"Yes, it's true, honey," I said as I lowered Lulu's hand. "But, it's not polite to point. When a woman has a baby her body creates milk in her breasts so she can feed her baby."

"Mama, is it true that I also drank milk from your boobies?"

"Yes, honey, you did," I said, hoping that would be the end of it. It wasn't.

"Just like a baby cow," Lulu giggled.

"Uhm, well, yes, I guess so," I said, trying to squeeze that image out of my head.

"Can I try it again right now?" she asked.

"What? No, you absolutely cannot," I said. "Uhm, let's go get some gelato." Lulu, of course, loves gelato and I had to get this subject changed, and changed quickly.

But, besides the impossibility of her last question, this exchange was the first time I recalled Lulu using the word "boobie" for "breast." Where'd she get that? I honestly don't remember when, or if, I made a conscious decision to describe a woman's breasts as "boobies" in front of Lulu. I don't call them that myself. "Boobs" maybe, sometimes, but never "boobies."

Yet, I must've been the one who started it. I'm sure Lulu didn't get that word from her Italian-speaking classmates in preschool. Maybe it was because the word "breasts"—with that "s" plus "t" plus "s" sound—can be pretty tricky for a little kid to say. Or maybe there had been some other reason. I don't know. "Boobies" does sound like a friendly kiddie word, like "binky" for "blanket."

It reminds me a little of how the comic George Carlin felt about the word "tits," claiming that they sounded "like a snack. 'New Nabisco Tits!'" I imagine tits would be like those small Cheez-it crackers. "Boobies" might be some kind of a Hostess cupcake-like treat. Like "Ding -Dongs." Never mind.

But since that fountainhead moment at the fountain, Lulu now says "boobie" so much that I'm used to it. "Boobie" is the word.

Many experts say parents should use the official words when they speak to their child about private parts from the get-go—the same way you tell your child that a "leg" is a "leg" and not, say, a "gam." But, maybe it's because there aren't that many nicknames for legs and there are lots of nicknames for our privates that compels us to ease into the more clinical-sounding "breasts," "vagina," or "penis" after some time. I don't know.

When Lulu was three, for instance, and in preschool in Baltimore, she came home one evening and announced that she knew "boys have 'peanuts.'" We let it stand. Even now, after providing the proper term a number of times, she still pronounces it pretty close to "peanuts."

But back to "boobies." Eventually I did take some time to give Lulu the more appropriate word. I sat her on my lap on the couch one evening and told her it was more polite to say "breasts."

"Oh, and don't forget that they are to be considered 'private,'" I added.

"Right, so, nobody should touch anyone's *boobies*," she said, emphasizing her point by poking at each of my breasts with her index finger while she talked. Then she chopped her hand karate-style between my breasts and added, "Except right here in the middle where there isn't a boobie. You can touch there."

"Okay, that's enough," I said. "Get down."

I don't think I have any major hang-ups with all this private stuff, really. I'm no prude, and I do believe that when a kid asks a straight-forward and honest question, they deserve a straight-forward and honest answer. So, later on, when Lulu dragged my box of feminine hygiene accessories out and asked what they were, you might think I was able to tell her about them quite matter-of-factly.

But, no, I didn't. I wasn't prepared at all.

I flashed back to how my own mom had deployed some sort of analogy to a chicken laying eggs and then if that egg wasn't fertilized, etc., etc., that had completely weirded me out. (First Lulu's cow analogy, and now my mom's chicken metaphor? Enough with the farm animals already!) So, I dodged Lulu's question and rushed online to a mother's group I am part of to ask them for advice. I received some good answers, and the next time Lulu inquired, I sweated a bit, and then dove into my well-rehearsed reply that involved a combination of science and glossing over. I still thought it sounded too graphic for my four-year-old to hear. I clenched my teeth, waiting for her reaction.

But she just casually replied, "Okay, I wanna go scooter now."

So much for my sweat, but at least I had avoided mentioning chickens.

The bidet that's next to our toilet in our home has also posed a bit of an explanation challenge. Every house and apartment here in Italy has one, but I hadn't thought about it before we moved, so again, I was unprepared. The day we arrived in Arezzo, Lulu tore through every room exploring. When she entered the bathroom, she took one look at the bidet and immediately turned on its little faucet. Water shot out.

"Look!" she yelled, elated. "A tiny sink! Just my size!"

I figured maybe it could be a great way to encourage her to wash her hands more often and did not offer her the alternative usage. Hearing about my ruse, a British buddy of mine clucked that "no self-respecting European" would let their child misuse a bidet like that.

But my dear friend Silvia, who lives down the street with a daughter the same age as Lulu, confided that none of the Italian moms she knows uses them in the traditional way.

"We all set our kids' toothpaste and toothbrush holders on the edge," she said. "Helps them remember to brush their teeth."

I'm an American gal, so Lulu can have the bidet all to herself. As for Lulu's lady parts, well, I saw the *Vagina Monologues* years ago in Manhattan, and I am all for calling 'em as I see 'em, as I've already said. But "vagina" seemed just too...too...I don't know. *Too.*

When Lulu was a baby, I settled on an upbeat-sounding word that I thought was an endearing Spanish version of it. "*Chucha*" sounds cute, right? Only after I had been using that word regularly around her for years did I go back and do the proper research and discover to my chagrin that the word is indeed Spanish in origin.

However, while it may *sound* very nice, it is actually the Spanish equivalent of a certain, vulgar English language C-word that I would never use. Great. It's also very close to the Italian word for "pacifier," *ciuccio.* Awkward.

So, I have since tried to teach Lulu the proper term for her lower extremities, but she still insists on calling her vagina a "chucha," much the way she still refers to her breasts as "boobies."

I unintentionally continued my international, vulgar linguistic education during a playdate at Lulu's friend Letizia's house.

Lulu and Letizia were standing before a large dollhouse using toy mice figurines as the family who lived inside. Letizia's mother Marika and I were sitting nearby, watching and trying to chat. I say "trying," because Marika speaks no English and my Italian is way below par.

Referencing the figurines the girls were playing with, I pointed to the one in Letizia's hand.

"That little mouse must be the daddy," I said. "Because I just heard Letizia call it "*topolino*," which is a male mouse, right?"

"*Buon lavoro*," Marika replied. "A male mouse is called a *topolino*."

"And the mommy, or female mouse, then, must be called a *topolina*," I added, trying to make what I thought would be an obvious connection.

"Baah!" Marika laughed and shook her head. "Oh no! You must never say *that* word. That's a naughty Italian word for..." And she pointed to her crotchal region.

What? Really? Oh, okay. That must explain then, why here in Italy Mickey Mouse is known as "*Topolino*" while Minnie Mouse is known simply as "Minnie."

Which, come to think of it, sounds just as cute as "boobie."

◆ ◆ ◆ ◆ ◆ ◆ ◆ ◆ ◆

*"But how does the baby get in
the mommy's tummy?"*

◆ ◆ ◆ ◆ ◆ ◆ ◆ ◆ ◆

FOURTEEN

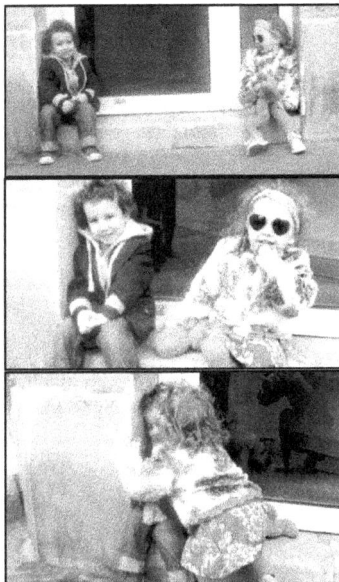

A MANY SPLENDORED THING

◆　◆　◆　◆　◆　◆　◆　◆　◆　◆

LULU NEVER MET A BOY SHE DIDN'T LOVE

L ULU HAS NEVER GONE THROUGH the *cooties* phase with boys.

We were exploring the medieval village of Castiglion Fiorentino one Saturday. A steep, winding cobblestone pathway led us under an ancient crest-topped archway toward the town's tower. As we hiked toward it, the skies darkened. It began to drizzle and then to pour. Lulu and I ducked into a tiny coffee shop to wait it out. Four or five elderly men were seated along the wall on our right and nodded to us—especially to Lulu, who was trying to close her green frog umbrella. The barista turned around from his dishwashing to tell Lulu he had a son about her age. Then he leaned over the counter, smiled, and asked Lulu a question.

I didn't understand what he asked since it was in fast-paced Italian, but the row of old men chuckled. Then they started to roar as Lulu began her answer by looking down at her hand and counting off names on her fingers.

"Tomaso… Leonardo… Luca… David… and Alessio."

The barista tilted his head back and joined the old men in laughter.

"Lulu!" I raised my eyebrows in surprise. "Did he just ask you how many boyfriends you have?"

"Uh-huh!" Lulu looked up at me beaming. "And I have a lot!"

Ziiing! A flashcard deck of memories flipped through my mind. The first ultrasound photo of Lulu where we could clearly see her upturned nose and tiny mouth. That pink and blue, little striped-knit stocking cap the nurses put on her newborn head. Her first teetery steps in Paris. Her first word. The time a random lady came up to us during our first family trip to the mall. She peered at tiny Lulu in the Baby Bjorn carrier on Scotty's shoulders and said, "Oooh! Enjoy your time. They grow up so fast."

And ziiing again! Back here I was to the present with Lulu just four years old and already talking about juggling boyfriends. The lady had been prophetic. It *was* fast. Too fast.

It all started with Alec. When Lulu was about two and we were living in Paris, her best friend was not a little girl, but a gorgeous three-year-old boy named Alec. He had dark curly hair, big brown eyes, and a lopsided smile that you just knew was going to make the ladies swoon. His mom Dana and I would meet up with our kids at a different park around town each week. Parc Monceau, with its Greek-like columns encircling a pond, is where Lulu and Alec shared *chocolats chauds* (hot chocolates). They twirled around on a giant yellow cowboy hat at Jardin du Luxembourg. And at the Jardin des Tuileries, Alec and Lulu bounced on trampolines. Other Parisian visitors may know the Musee d'Osay or the Louvre, but I am a former resident expert on kiddie attractions.

After only her second date—make that *play* date—Lulu slid over and kissed Alec (on the cheek) before she left. She had to take her purple *tétine* (pacifier) out of her mouth first, but Alec didn't seem to mind.

A year later, when we moved back to the US, the little lovebirdies sent cards back and forth with crayon drawings and toddler-scrawled signatures. Lulu received a new stuffed puppy-dog and named it "Alec" in his honor. She told me, "I will marry the real Alec when I grow up." Back in Paris, Dana's mom emailed me that Alec had started to refuse his afternoon snacks, saying he wanted to put the money into his piggy bank instead. The reason why became clear when he later asked Dana: "How many pennies will it take to buy an airplane ticket to see Lulu?"

Last fall, we used our own pennies and flew back to Paris to visit them. Lulu and Alec had a terrific reunion playing together and just being friends. She didn't try to kiss him and didn't mention marriage to me. I soon realized it wasn't because she had passed through a phase; it was because she has a new stable of potential future-husbands closer to home.

I took stock of Lulu's list at the coffee shop. I figured I didn't have to worry that much about Tomaso and Leonardo. They were both five-year-olds, a big year ahead of Lulu, and about to graduate from Bianca Maria Bianchini preschool and move along. Luca is the eldest son of my friend Chay, who we see all the time, but since he's eleven, I think he's busier playing guitar and taking Judo lessons than reciprocating Lulu's admiration. (His little brother Jack is enamored with Lulu. But, poor thing, I noticed he didn't make the list.) David happens to be Lulu's same age and they are also in the same class at school, but his mother Pavlina and I have watched them playing together, and we agree they're just buddies.

Ah, that leaves Alessio. Let's see what I think of him. In spite of his Italian name, he's one of two sons of our American friends Charlotte and Kirk, who run the campus of Oklahoma University here in Arezzo. Fluent in English and Italian, Alessio is a sweet-hearted, violin-playing boy with a singing voice like an angel that could rival anyone in the Vienna Boys Choir. All right. I approve. He's a good one to be on the list. I won't have Scotty get out the shotgun.

The next week, Lulu and I met Alessio and his brother Max at the park, Parco Il Prato. They ran around together playing tag, not doctor. So far, so good. On Thursday, we walked over to their comfortable brick and stone home for a spaghetti dinner. We were joined by a group of friends, and after dinner we all walked across the street to cheer Alessio on at his violin recital at the old seminary near Arezzo's *duomo,* or cathedral. The recital was that terrific mix of kids who were musically gifted; and kids, like I had been, who were not. Fortunately for Alessio, he fell in the former category. Even though he was just a beginner, he sustained his notes perfectly, and I think I even detected a warm vibrato. Lulu was impressed.

"I am really in love with Alessio," Lulu told me on the way back home.

"Okay, then," I said, nervously testing the waters, "what does love mean exactly to you, Lulu?"

"Love is two people married," Lulu said. "Love is also super good toys and friends."

Well, okay, the second half sounded like we were maybe talking about the same thing. I decided I would focus on the "good toys and friends" part.

My first "boyfriend" had also been a good friend. Todd and I were the top two readers in Mrs. Sholley's third grade class and we played four-square together at every single recess. Our parents, friends, and teachers knew us as a little "couple." And I think we were. But we were also chaste. We only held hands once that I can remember during a school field trip to the planetarium in Muncie, Indiana. All that sitting in the dark and all.

"Right, Lulu," I said trying to direct her emotions, "Alessio is a really nice boy and you like him a lot, just like a toy or a friend."

"Yes, but, Mama," Lulu added, "I love him the most of anyone ever."

"What is it you love about him, exactly?" I asked.

"He plays lovely music," Lulu said.

She had a point there. I sympathized with her attraction to the artistic types. On the first day that I met her father, he recited poetry to me—pages and pages of memorized verse. It worked like a charm and I was head over heels. But by then I was much older than when I had that first boyfriend in third grade. And even then, I was a *very* mature eight-year -old, whereas Lulu is only half that.

I dropped the subject and didn't think any more about it until the next time we were off to dinner at Charlotte and Kirk's. Lulu had me stop along our walk because she wanted to "pick flowers for Alessio."

When we arrived at their gate, Alessio and several other friends' children were already playing outside. It was a warm summer evening with the scent of jasmine in the air from the bush along the front walk, which sat next to terracotta pots filled with pink petunias and red geraniums. Slices of *salami* and a bowl of *fave fresche* (delicious Italian green beans that you open and eat raw, because Italian cuisine without beans is like American cuisine without ketchup) were placed on a table in the yard.

The romantic atmosphere was perfect and Lulu climbed smiling out of her *passeggino* and headed straight toward Alessio with her bouquet. Jack ran up and intercepted her. He gave her a tiny perfume spray. She took it, and after spraying her neck like she's seen me do, told me it would make her smell "more lovelier for Alessio." Lord. Jack didn't seem to be aware of the slight and just ran off to catch up with the other kids. Lulu went back to tracking down Alessio. When he noticed her, he quickly turned away and ran upstairs into the house.

"Uh-oh," I thought, "he's probably embarrassed by Lulu's overt display of affection. That could be a good thing."

But he just as quickly reappeared carrying what looked like a giant Valentine. It was a big stretch of red construction paper crookedly cut into the shape of a heart. Alessio took Lulu's flowers very graciously and then presented her with his art work. He had written on it, "Lulu, you are very funny and cute. You look like a princess and smell like a rose. Love,

Alessio."

Hold it. Hold everything. What?! This kid's not embarrassed at all! In fact, he likes—no, wait—he *loves* her too. That's it. That's. It! Back when my little elementary school boyfriend Todd had tried to give me a tiny heart-shaped bottle of toilet water for Valentine's Day, my mom promptly made me return it to him, telling me, "You're too young to receive gifts from boys."

Lulu was even younger. Maybe I shouldn't let her keep the heart. Maybe I should call Scotty to get out that shotgun after all. But before I could think of what to say, Cassandra came trotting over to see what was going on. She is a couple of years older than Lulu and the beautiful, blue-eyed, long-haired daughter of our friend Heather, a California blonde married to a gregarious Italian named Stefano.

Lulu looked up at Cassandra and announced, "Alessio gave me this and I love him."

Alessio, clearly enjoying the attention, said to Lulu, "So, if you love me, you want to give me a kiss?"

My little baby Lulu, who just yesterday was wearing that maternity ward pink and blue stocking cap, didn't even hesitate.

I was standing nearby just watching and listening to all this with my mouth open, but no sounds coming out. Alessio leaned forward. Lulu moved toward him. She puckered up her lips and planted them on his… cheek.

Well, thank goodness.

I didn't want to step in and make a big deal about it, but I also didn't think I should just sit idly by. I hadn't imagined I would be dealing with any of this boy stuff at just four years old. At eight, sure, fine, but not at four. I was still standing there slack-jawed, when Cassandra, who had also been looking on, nonchalantly remarked, "Oh, I've kissed him, too. C'mon, Lulu, let's go play."

Lulu tossed me the heart and grabbed Cassandra's hand, and the three of them went skipping off to play. Just like that. The end. I decided to let her keep the Valentine. It's taped up inside the door of her armoire in her bedroom. I am resigned to the fact it's the beginning of many more to come.

◆　◆　◆　◆　◆　◆　◆　◆　◆

"I love you and Daddy, but
Nutella I really love."

◆　◆　◆　◆　◆　◆　◆　◆　◆

FIFTEEN

A SONG IN HER HEART

WHEN MORE THAN MUSIC COMES OUT

LULU TURNED TO ME the other day and announced, "We learned a song about a rainbow at school today. I would sing it for you, but you wouldn't understand. It's in Italian."

Sadly, she's probably right.

Like many children her age, Lulu loves to sing. When we're on our walks to the park or to school, or trudging the long way back home, Lulu often lifts up her head from her stroller and chirps out a non-stop concert for me and whomever we pass by. Whether they are real songs, ad-libbed ditties, or random snippets from kids' TV shows, Lulu can usually be heard belting out some tune. The *nonni*, or grandmas and grandpas, who live in our neighborhood have grown so accustomed to our melodious meanderings, they now call out, *"Che cosa è la canzone per oggi* (What's the song for today)?" And lately Lulu has been singing about a caterpillar, a ladybug, or that aforementioned *arcobaleno* (rainbow).

That's because the bugs and the rainbow are part of a series of songs about a morning in a meadow taught by her preschool's dynamic music teacher. Scotty and I watched their performance at a school dinner recently. Dressed in navy and white, the kids assembled in front of a green paper backdrop with a giant butterfly, ladybug, sun, rainbow, and top hat-wearing caterpillar pasted on. They opened their mouths (the kids, not the creatures) and yelled/sang the tunes of the meadow. It sounded great. We just didn't understand a whole lot. Funny, too, because the first songs Lulu learned to sing weren't even in Italian, but in another language I don't fully comprehend: French.

My friend Laurence, who lived just down the street from us in Paris near Rue de la Convention, taught us our first French song. With two daughters older than Lulu, Rosalie and Carole, Laurence was an experienced teacher. Once I learned it, before Lulu was even a year old, I would raise my arms up bent at the elbow and sing:

> *"Ainsi font, font, font,*
> *Les petites marionnettes,*
> *Ainsi font, font, font,*
> *Trois p'tits tours et puis s'en vont."*

> "And so, do, do, do like this,
> The little puppets,
> And so, do, do, do, like this,
> Three little turns and then they leave."

You see, your hands become the *marionnettes*. You twist and turn and then zip your hands behind your back to match the words. Lulu used to giggle and wave her hands every time I'd sing it. It's a traditional French song without anything comparable in English that I know of.

But I later learned, quite by accident, that many of our English children songs have charming French equivalents. It was at a party at Lulu's nursery Ribambelle. Scotty and I were sitting in the back of the room when one of the teachers asked us to sing an English children's song. I agreed, but as I was caught off-guard, I didn't pick anything elaborate—just the first one that popped into my mind.

"The itsy-bitsy spider went up the waterspout.
Down came the rain and washed the spider out.
Up came the sun and dried up all the rain,
And the itsy-bitsy spider went up the spout again."

Naturally, I did the hand motions and everything. The French teachers all laughed and said they knew that one. I was surprised. Only one of these teachers spoke fluent English. How could they? Then Rodolfo, Lulu's favorite teacher, started to beat on a drum and everyone sang in unison—same tune, different words:

*"La toute petite araignée a grimpé le long de la gouttière.
La pluie est tombée et a emporté l'araignée.
Le soleil s'est levé et a séché toute la pluie,
Et la toute petite araignée a regrimpé le long de la gouttière."*

I noticed they had to rush a bit to squeeze their more syllabled French words to fit the original music's cadence, but what I really noticed, and what surprised me, was that Lulu sang right along to this version and seemed to know the French words better than what I sang with her.

There was one special traditional French children's song that Lulu and I both learned the words to together. We practiced all the time and had a private performance for Scotty. It was, and still is, my very favorite: *"Une Souris Verte."* It's a completely nonsensical story about someone who finds a green mouse and grabs it by the tail. The finder then shows it to some men who advise dunking it in water and oil. Then the mouse turns into a warm snail.

*"Une souris verte
Qui courait dans l'herbe
Je l'attrape par la queue,
Je la montre à ces messieurs
Ces messieurs me disent :
Trempez-la dans l'huile,
Trempez-la dans l'eau,
Ça fera un escargot
Tout chaud."*

"A green mouse
Who's running in the grass,
I grab it by the tail.
I show it to some gentlemen.
The gentlemen tell me,

'Dunk it in the oil,
Dunk it in the water,
It will become a snail,
Nice and warm.'"

Swear to God. I couldn't make that up. That really is what happens in the song. On your next visit to Paris, look around in the children's stores. You'll see books, stuffed animals, and lots and lots of references to the "green mouse." Every French person knew this song, but no one could tell me anything about its origins or its meaning. Why is the mouse green and why does it turn into a snail? Maybe because the French are so fond of eating nice and warm *escargots*? I have no idea, but anyway, I absolutely love it.

When we got back to the States, we started focusing on some American standards.

Even before Lulu was born, Scotty and I had compiled a list of songs we imagined singing together as a family on long road trips across the United States. Scotty suggested great old classics like "Sixteen Tons" and the very appropriate song for highway wandering, "King of the Road." I came up with more child-like offerings like "Twinkle, Twinkle, Little Star" and "I've Been Workin' on the Railroad." We pictured the two of us in the front seat driving past beautiful countryside. our merry little munchkin strapped in the backseat. All of us singing together. Like the VonTrapps, but not so many. And now, after Paris, that we were back in the US and she was a little older, it seemed like the perfect time to begin teaching songs from the list to Lulu.

She quickly picked up "Twinkle, Twinkle, Little Star," but definitely preferred the slightly creepier version that Scotty taught her, "Twinkle, Twinkle, Little Bat." She also latched onto "I've Been Workin' on the Railroad," which got extra teaching support as it was also a favorite at her preschool in our new home city of Baltimore. One evening as she was splashing in her bath, I heard her singing it on her own in her three-year-old style with missed words and those still soft-r's: "I been *woohkin'* on the *waaail-woooad* all the live-long daaaay." She sounded like Elmer Fudd.

She later marched into the living room and sat at her toy piano. Placing her hands over the keyboard, I think she must've thought the correct tune to match her vocal efforts would just magically resound from her instrument. After a moment or two of pounding on the piano and loudly singing the "Wailwoad" song, Lulu abruptly stopped.

"Mama!" Lulu hollered. "My piano's not working right. The music does not go with my song. 'I Been Woohkin' on the Wailwoad' does NOT sound right at all."

It didn't sound right with or without the piano accompaniment, I thought, considering those cute little soft r's.

"Well, Lulu," I said, "why don't you sing another song instead?"

"Okay," Lulu said, "I know 'Twinkle Twinkle' and all the good songs. But 'Woohkin' on the Wailwoad' has too many words."

She forgot about trying to play the piano for a while and sang a couple of songs a capella. She sang "Twinkle"—both star and bat versions—"Zippa-dee-doo-dah," and a song that she made-up: something about water and a clock. Occasionally she would sit down again at her piano and plunk out a few random notes, not appearing to mind any more that the tune wasn't matching the words. Scotty was in the dining room, and once in a while Lulu would get up from her chair at the little piano and skip over to him singing, "And I hop and run and I hop and run..." Then she would return to her piano and plink around a little more. And then back to Dad. I marveled at the freedom of expression and joyful imagination she was sharing with us. It was a truly sweet and fleeting moment.

I was sitting there smiling at her when she stopped and seemed to understand my expression. "When I do nice things, it makes your heart get bigger, doesn't it, Mama?" Lulu observed.

Such insight in the midst of all the skipping and singing. "Yes, indeed," I told her. "Yes, indeed."

She skip-hopped over to her daddy and said, "If you like, I will go everywhere you go and then I will make noise."

Okay, maybe not such tremendous insight after all.

We arrived in Italy a year later with plenty of American preschool favorites memorized and ready to embrace the Italian substitutes. But, not surprisingly, Lulu's local preschool didn't focus on reheating American tunes into Italian. They focused on wonderful traditional Italian children songs instead. My favorite is one that Lulu now sings all the time. It's about a "beautiful laundress" who washes handkerchiefs, then inexplicably jumps up and down and turns around and finally gives someone a kiss. There are great hand motions that accompany this tune. For example, when the lovely laundry gal is cleaning the hankies, the kids all kneel on the ground moving their clenched hands up and down across their thighs like they're scrubbing on a washboard. Lulu has never seen a washboard in use before, except maybe in some American bluegrass band, but there she is merrily rubbing along.

"La bella lavanderina
Che lava i fazzoletti
Per i poveretti
Della città.

Fai un salto,
Fanne un altro.
Fai la giravolta,
Fai un'altra volta.
Guarda in su,
Guarda in giù.
Dai un bacio
A chi vuoi tu."

"The beautiful laundress
Who's washing the handkerchiefs
For the poor
In the city.
Make a jump,
Make another.
Make a turn,
Make another turn.
Look up,
Look down.
Give a kiss
To whomever you want."

When she's at her school singing this song, the kids apparently take turns leading the motions, and then whomever they kiss at the end gets to lead the next round of singing. Lulu told me she always kisses Leonardo. He's one of the many little boys she talks about all the time. One of her so-called "boyfriends." Egads.

Finally, just last month, we came across an Italian version of an American favorite. A lively rendition of "Old MacDonald," with a few notable differences. In Italy, there is no mention of anyone named Mac-Donald; rather we're visiting with Uncle Tobia instead. And he apparently isn't old either. It's his farm (*fattoria*) that has the age issue:

"Nella vecchia fattoria, Ia-Ia-Oh
Quante bestie ha zio Tobia, Ia-Ia-Oh
C'è la mucca (MUU),

C'è la mucca (MUU),
(MUU), (MUU), (MUU), (MUU), (MUU),
Nella vecchia fattoria, Ia-Ia-Oh."

Here's how it would directly translate into English, which of course doesn't have the same rhyme or musical lilt:

"In the old farm, E-I-E-I-O,
How many animals does Uncle Tobia have? E-I-E-I-O
There's a (insert type of animal here).
The (type of animal) says (and now make its sound)
In the old farm, E-I-E-I-O."

It was fairly easy for me to learn and so I was delighted when Lu-lu and I began to sing it together recently, as we drove along from Tuscany to the more northern Emilia-Romagna region. It was like my earlier dream of us all singing together as a family on a good old-fashioned American road trip.

Except we weren't in America. Oh, and Scotty wasn't with us. He was out of town that weekend. We were with our friend Charlotte and her two young boys Max and Alessio instead. (As Charlotte's husband was also out of town, we were taking the kids to the annual International Street Performers' Festival in the mountain village of Pennabilli.) Oh, and since these were roads going through mountains, there were plenty of hair-pin turns and switch-backs, nothing like driving along the grand stretches of highway through the American plains that I had been picturing. Oh, and have I mentioned that Lulu had pretty serious motion sickness around this time? She did. And although I had packed sick-sacs in anticipation, I couldn't get them out of my bag's pocket in time.

So, while we were singing *"Nella vecchia fattoria,"* she threw up. All over.

Max and Alessio, who were sitting on either side of her, were grossed out. Charlotte had to pull over the van along the side of some twisty road so we could change Lulu's soaked clothes and wipe down the car. (I was briefly reminded of the *bella lavanderina* song, but neither Lulu, nor I, was feeling very *bella* at that moment.) At least we had managed to sing a little. Albeit without Daddy. In Italy. In between vomiting.

Actually, it wasn't like my pre-conceived vision of the American family-road-trip-sing-along at all.

♦ ♦ ♦ ♦ ♦ ♦ ♦ ♦ ♦

LULU: *"Sing me that song about the silly mice."*
ME: *"Uhm, what song, exactly?"*
LULU: *"You know, 'Three BLONDE Mice.'"*

♦ ♦ ♦ ♦ ♦ ♦ ♦ ♦ ♦

SIXTEEN

ALL YOU CAN EAT
YOUR GOOSE IS COOKED WHEN
THE GOOSE IS THE COOK

IMAGINE A CARTOON WHITE GOOSE wearing a big, floppy chef's hat. Now imagine that it sings—in Italian, of course—as it teaches you how to make meatballs or *spaghetti alla carbonara* or the traditional Tuscan dish of *Panzanella*.

Great. You're now watching *Cuocarina* with Lulu and me. It's the name of a television series of animated shorts on Italy's RAI Yoyo kids' channel, inserted like a commercial between programs. Italians confirm for me that it's not an official Italian word, more likely a blend between *cuoca* (cook) and *ocarina* (little goose). Whatever its origin, Lulu and I love to sing along with the singing goose chef as it warbles, "*Cuocarina! Cuocarina!*" during its mini-cooking show.

It also makes perfect sense that *ricette*, or recipes, are the equivalent of public service announcements for children in Italy, because cooking is more than a way of life here; cooking *is* life.

Gelato is so ubiquitous Lulu just takes it for granted. Her favorites are *fragola* (strawberry), *cioccolato* (chocolate), *limone* (lemon), and *zucchero filato* (cotton candy), which tastes exactly like the name and is waaay too sweet for me. Pastas come in so many different shapes, like *gemelli, stringozzi,* and *strozzapreti* (the last one meaning "priest stranglers"), that we could never hope to try them all.

There are hand-made *biscotti* (cookies) with almond slices or orange peel from *Senora* Ada, who runs our favorite bakery La Magia del Grano, and who gives Lulu an extra cookie every time we come in. And peasant-style rustic breads. Delicious. Ada bakes a variety of these, of which *schiarcciata* is Lulu's and my favorite by far. The flatbread is soft with dimples and in Tuscany it is drizzled in olive oil and sprinkled with salt. Frida, the extraordinary cook at Lulu's preschool (where the kids eat as well as any American tourist could ever hope to in an expensive *ristorante*), passes slices of it around every morning to the children as part of their daily *colazione*, or breakfast.

Lulu's passion for this Italian bread reminds me of when she was about eleven months old in Paris. Scotty was making dinner, so I carried our baby in my arms with me as I left our apartment to walk across the street to the closest *boulangerie* for a *baguette*. I'd been there several times before, but this was the first time there was a long queue snaking outside the bread shop's doors. The aroma coming from within convinced me to stay. When it was my turn, I asked for "*une baguette s'il vous plait*," and instantly realized why so many people were waiting. The bread was hot. Fresh from the oven. Incredible. Lulu, with only about four teeth in her head, couldn't resist the fragrant temptation either. She lunged forward and sank those four teeth, like tiny fangs, into the *baguette*. But her little chompers couldn't wrestle the chunk away from the loaf, so she pushed her face against the crust and kind of gnawed at it like a baby beaver stuck to its first tree. The group of usually reserved Parisian customers howled.

Of course, babies, who have now become preschoolers, can't live on bread alone (although here in Italy, it could easily be argued otherwise), so we're lucky to also have the bounty from Tuscany's nutrient-rich soil. You could certainly live more than well enough here simply on fruits and veggies. Out in the countryside, where our home is, for example, we are surrounded on three sides by large *orti*, or vegetable gardens.

Luciano has the most impressive plot. We see him out there every day, starting in the cold month of February, turning the dirt with only a shovel, a pitchfork, and a hoe. Nothing is mechanical; it's all by hand. He even draws his water from a well on the property. This soft-spoken elderly man is always alone, too. He never has a helper. But *piano piano* (little by little) he transforms that bare soil into a patchwork of produce perfection. It's truly beautiful to behold. There are tidy rows of leafy Swiss chard, alternating with purple eggplants that he places straw around to hold in moisture, a rectangular section of yellow squash, perfect columns of one of Lulu's favorite vegetables, *piselli* (peas), and a booming batch of white flowered bushes surely teeming with roots full of potatoes underneath. His garden is organized and symmetrical. There are flawless narrow dirt paths and irrigation trenches that outline the produce patches like the seams in a quilt.

As my Italian has gotten better, I've been able to learn more about Luciano's endeavors. He doesn't grow everything for his family, for example. One morning as we passed him sitting under a tree, peeling back the green stems and tying together bunches of garlic, he informed us that he sold these bundles to markets around town. Interesting, I thought. Lulu whispered that the sun-dried white clusters looked like "bunches of bones." Even more interesting, I thought.

Our hospitable neighbors like Luciano have given us armloads of fresh vegetables: zucchini, peppers, greens, and tomatoes. Okay, I know tomatoes are technically fruit. The neighbors have given us loads of those, too. We've eaten succulent peaches, cherries red as oxblood, and there are fig trees along every path and street on which we walk. We pick them green and soft right from the branch. Lulu has expanded her fruity repertoire far beyond her former single favorite of bananas.

The rich Tuscan soil yields some of the juiciest, deep red strawberries I've ever seen. And *cocomero* (which is the regional Aretino word for watermelon). Well, I don't think Lulu ever really appreciated the bland watery ones she had eaten before. But now, she loves them so much, she doesn't even mind picking out the seeds. Tuscans are purists. Seedless watermelons just don't exist here. Lulu has categorized fruit into two groups.

"I like every fruit that is like strawberries, but I really extremely like wah-der-meh-lun!" she says, drawing out each syllable for emphasis.

But in addition to the fruity confections, with some guidance from that singing goose chef, Lulu and I one day decided to experiment with making Italian sweet treats that required some cooking to help them along.

The experiment was not a success.

While dads in America may enjoy pancakes in bed on Father's Day, here in Italy, the holiday calls for *frittelle di riso*, or rice fritters. Lulu brought some home from school in a little decorated bag on March 19th.

La Festa del Babbo, or Father's Day, is celebrated in March, not in June as in the U.S., because the date coincides with Saint Joseph's feast day, who is feted as the father of *Gesù*. Well, earthly father anyway. The fritters were crispy on the outside and light, fluffy, and sweet like rice pudding on the inside. Scrumptious. We saved them for *Babbo* (Tuscan for "Daddy"), but since there were only six of them and each was only about the size of a two-Euro coin (roughly the same as a fifty-cent piece), we were still hungry for more.

I was searching on the internet for a recipe, when *Cuocarina* came on the "tee-voo" (the letter "v" is pronounced "voo" in Italian). The goose was singing and squawking about how to make the holiday's *frittelle*. Lulu and I sang with him as I jotted down the ingredients and instructions. Then, with Lulu's help, we proceeded to make the crunchiest, gummiest, most awful-tasting fritters ever. They were sweet dirt clods. Blech.

"Mama, I don't think you did it right," Lulu pointed out.

"Yeah," I more than readily agreed, "these don't taste at all like the ones they helped you make at school."

"No, they taste yucky. Let's throw them in the *cestino*," Lulu said. (*Cestino* means "garbage can," as if you had to have me tell you that considering the trash-worthy result.)

I have a better touch with more familiar American-style cooking and baking. Tuscany, while good with pasta, bread, and *biscotti*, is not known for its light and fluffy pastries. They generally offer dense *torte* (pies) or flaky pastries in their *pasticcerie* (bakeries). So Lulu gets pretty excited when I decide to make an old-fashioned cake. Sometimes she doesn't wait until I decide.

One day this winter, Lulu apparently woke up with a sweet-tooth. Still lying in her bed, she bellowed in a very demanding voice, "Mama! Make me a banana cake!"

"Lulu, we don't have time. It's time to get up and get ready for school," I called back.

"If you don't do it," she yelled, remaining in her room, "your consequence will be I won't walk with you." And if that wasn't enough, she added, "I'll still be your daughter, but I'll hide all day under the covers."

I didn't make the cake. Not then anyway. And she eventually did come out from under her blankets and made it to school.

Lulu has much better luck when it comes to ordering pasta from her dad. He's almost always prepared to professionally roll out a fresh batch. Interestingly, Scotty first started pasta-making when we lived in France, not here in Italy. He purchased a cookbook by a chef from the Tuscan town of Lucca, which we took with us to Paris. From *tagliatelle* to *tortelli di zucca*, Scotty makes terrific pasta *fatto a mano* (by hand). I think having a human and not a goose as your cooking mentor is a much wiser choice.

Lulu turns on a pretend "tee-voo" in our kitchen when she's assisting one of us. She proceeds to host her own little cooking show. "Hello everyone!" she says. "Today we are making pasta! I am the sous-chef and Daddy is the boss-chef."

Scotty rolls out the dough to a thickness that is practically transparent. Lulu pushes out her own little dough-ball to a whole inch or so thick, pressing it into shapes with cookie cutters. Hers resemble lumpy biscuits rather than thin strips of lasagna.

Lulu gobbles up all of Scotty's pasta offerings, even the fiery flavors of *pasta puttanesca*, which was apparently named in honor of Italy's ladies of the evening who tossed in every savory item from their pantries to create this appropriately spicy and lusty sauce.

Her favorite right now is *pasta al pesto*. She just goes crazy for pesto sauce. She'll ask for it by name in restaurants. And even if it's not written on the menu, every kitchen seems to have the supplies on-hand, so she has never been disappointed. I love it that I have a kid who is not afraid to eat noodles with something more than a little butter. Although, like every kid, she occasionally eats her noodles plain, too. Here they call it *pasta bianca*, which literally means "white pasta." But instead of dousing the pasta with butter or margarine, Tuscans pour green virgin olive oil over it instead and sprinkle with a little *Parmigiano-Reggiano* cheese. Not exactly white.

Another green favorite in our home is crepes. Green? Why are they green and not ordinary creamy, yellow batter-colored? Because Lulu has discovered the joys of food-coloring, that's why. It started on St. Patrick's Day. Scotty is proudly of Irish descent, and as I was making the crepes that morning, Lulu asked if we could turn them green in his honor. She squeezed a few drops in, and they came out looking like large wafers of spinach.

"They look icky, Mama."

"Well, they'll taste good, I think," I said.

"They look like squished frogs."

Fortunately, the crepes tasted much better than they looked.

And, continuing to speak of the verdant hues of green, my personal, hands-down, number one favorite find of our time here in Tuscany is absolutely our discovery of *Olio Nuovo*. Our Tuscan neighbors started getting excited about it late last September. By mid-October, they were practically into a mad frenzy. *Olio Nuovo* is the first-press oil from just-picked green olives. That didn't mean so much to me, at first, when our Italian friends told us about it, drooling. I've tried lots of different kinds of olive oils in my life. Greek, Italian, Californian. What was the big deal?

Then we visited friends in Cortona who owned a small grove of olive trees. It was October, and Fabrizio and his wife Guisy had just bottled the first-press. He handed us a bottle of the brightest colored green liquid I had ever seen that wasn't radioactive. If I hadn't seen it myself, I wouldn't have believed this color could exist in nature.

I poured a little onto a white plate. It gleamed and glowed. I dabbed a little sour-dough bread into the puddle and put it into my mouth. Being from Indiana, all I can compare it to is the difference between milk from a store and fresh milk from a cow. The flavor was so pungently crisp and sharp, raw and original, that I was taken aback.

So was Lulu. "Blech. This tastes like grass," she said. We agreed to disagree. I thought, "No problem, more for me." Scotty and I liked it so much, we even drizzled it on vanilla ice cream with a little sprinkling of sea salt. *Che buona!*

Lulu can have the green crepes, and I'll stick to the fluorescent green of *Olio Nuovo*. I'm sure the goose would approve.

◆ ◆ ◆ ◆ ◆ ◆ ◆ ◆ ◆

"Happy birthday, Mama!
Can we have cake for breakfast since it's
your birthday?"

◆ ◆ ◆ ◆ ◆ ◆ ◆ ◆ ◆

SEVENTEEN

TUSCAN TRUE ROMANCE

◆ ◆ ◆ ◆ ◆ ◆ ◆ ◆ ◆ ◆

LULU NEVER MET A PIG SHE DIDN'T LIKE
—TO EAT

TUSCANY'S ONE TRUE LOVE is the pig. The way Parisians are enamored with cheese, here in Tuscany nearly everyone swoons over a piece of pork.

One of the most revered porcine delicacies is *porchetta*.
Grocery stores and markets announce the arrival of a new batch
by writing on chalk-boards placed outside the front doors or by
unfurling large pre-printed banners that proudly proclaim:
"*Porchetta Oggi* (Porchetta Today)!" But it's not for the squeamish.
Porchetta happens to be a suckling pig (poor thing), deboned, salt-
ed, and stuffed with its own liver, garlic, and spices. The skin is
very crispy and it's usually served up as a piglet sandwich.

I'm an admitted carnivore hypocrite, which means I eat

meat, but I don't like to think about where it came from. So maybe I'm too much of a wimp and couldn't get past the image of that sweet little talking piggy from the old movie *Babe*, or maybe I just didn't care for the texture of that layer of crispy fat that surrounds the spiced meat. Whatever the reason, I only tasted it once, and that was enough.

However, I am guiltily quite fond of many other tasty, Tuscan piggy treats. And so are many other people. So many, that entire sections of any grocery store or *bottega* are dedicated to those precious slivers of ham known as *prosciutto*. You'll not find just one metal arm of dangling plastic wrapped *prosciutto* packages like in the States. Here there is an abundance of variety. I have learned to distinguish among *proscuitto roto* (roasted), *prosciutto crudo* (cured), *prosciutto cotto* (plain old cooked), *prosciutto di Modena,* and *prosciutto di Parma.* The last two are types of *proscuitto* simply distinguished by the names of the town the piggies first hailed from. Maybe that explains Bologna. I never thought that perhaps my favorite childhood sandwich eaten between two slices of Roman Meal whole wheat bread (my mother would never have dreamed of buying gooey white Wonder bread) was based on a kind of pork meat originating from the Italian city of the same name. Or maybe they just named it that in the US to throw you off the track of what it's really made of. Anyway, the bologna-looking meat here in Italy is called *mortadella,* so who knows.

One thing you won't find here in pork-product-lunch-meat-land is any economy or family-sized packages. Each *prosciutto* vacuum-pack contains only three or four precious slices.

If you need to purchase more than that, you'll have to visit the butcher (*il macellaio*). Ours is named Andrea. He and his wife Nicoletta own the La Bottega di Via Tarlarti, which is just down the street from Lulu's school, and they couldn't be any nicer. They always greet us by name with a friendly "*Ciao!*" and then Nicoletta gives Lulu a piece of freshly made bread to munch on while we shop. Andrea stands behind the counter surrounded by giant dried and cured hog legs. Their cloven hooves are usually clipped off, but the rest of their leg and massive thigh bones are still intact. They're hanging overhead from hooks like so many petrified guitars. Andrea taught me that the legs which still have their little trotters are called *Prosciutto di San Daniele*, a specially cured kind of dried meat that is more sweet than salty. I just point and he carves me up some *fetti* (slices), as thick or as thin as I like. It's apparently been this way for hundreds of generations.

At a party in the small village of Pergo last summer, I was talking with a British anthropologist who had just written a book on the Etruscans, the ancient people who lived in this region. Researchers discovered an old hog slaughtering pit where discarded parts had been tossed tens of thousands of years ago. They found plenty of bits of bone, but not one single ham hip or shank among the lot. And the partial skeletons they did find down in that pit didn't belong to domesticated swine like we're used to, but more likely their larger and more burly cousins, the *cinghiale*, or wild boar.

We didn't know wild boar roamed our hills and fields before we moved here, but they sure do. There are estimated to be some 150,000 of the tusked razorbacks in Tuscany, and Lulu and I have seen their tracks along the path to her school on more than one occasion.

Thankfully, we've never met one face to face on the path. The only way we've seen one up close has been on our plates. Friends took us to a "*Sagra del Cinghiale*," or Feast of Wild Boar, about a month after we unpacked. We were in the rolling countryside outside of Cortona. Rows and rows of long banquet tables were set up in an open field under large white tents. We stood in line to buy our meal tickets with dozens of village locals; not only were we the only Americans in the place, but we were also the only people not completely familiar with this annual traditional custom. We had no idea, for example, that when Scotty bought two drink tickets for what we presumed would be two glasses of wine, the low-low price of just two Euro actually landed us two full *bottles* of *vino di rosso*.

So, as each of us contemplated our personal bottle of wine, we found some seats and began the feast. There was *cinghiale* steak, *cinghiale* sausage, and Lulu's favorite, *pappadelle al cinghiale*, which were wide, flat noodles with a chunky wild boar sauce ladled on top.

"More piggy! More Piggy!" Lulu delightedly, dare I say it, *squealed* as she asked for seconds. With her soft "r" pronunciation, it came out more like, "Mo' piggy! Mo' Piggy!" Her enthusiasm charmed our new friends and also the strangers seated with us at the long table. It also probably didn't hurt that Scotty was filling all the raised glasses around us with our plentiful wine. The whole experience was delicious and enchanting. Since then we've been to another delightful *Sagra*, where I learned that you can also buy wine by the glass for just fifty cents.

Lulu's love of eating *cinghiale* is only surpassed by her love for them as pets. Not a real one of course, but Scotty found a plush stuffed animal *cinghiale* at a store here in Arezzo, complete with soft little tusks and hooves, that Lulu regularly takes to school and sometimes sleeps with.

"His name is Konky, because he goes, 'Konk, Konk, Konk' with his big nose," she will explain in a nasally snort to anyone who asks.

Surpassing *pancetta* or *prosciutto*, or even the delicacy of the *cinghiale*, Lulu's everyday treat is *salumi* and *salami*. And no, I've not just typed the same thing two different ways. Here's a little Tuscan-piggy-pickiness I picked up: *salumi* and *salami* are not one in the same. *Salumi* is the general term for Italian-style preserved meats, and *salami* is a type of *salumi* due to the special way it's cured and fermented.

So, one day we walked into our *supermercato* and saw the grand-daddy of all *salumi* on display. I'm not exactly sure if it might also have been from the subset *salami*, but Lulu and I agreed that it was HUGE. To better paint this image, let me explain that I like to call this store "the Disco," because invariably there is some old dance party music thumping through its stereo system. And on this particular day, Rick James' classic "Super Freak" greeted us as the automatic glass doors slid open.

"She's a very kinky girl,
The kind you don't take home to mother..."

Lulu was laughing as I began bopping and singing along with Rick James while I pushed our cart. We first arrived at the pasta and bread aisles.

"She will never let your spirits down,
Once you get her off the street."

Then, we turned the corner to the fresh produce area to select some veggies.

"She's all right, she's all right,
That girl's all right, with me, yeah."

And then. Then it happened. We rounded into our final stop. The pork section. And there it was.

A ginormous, twelve foot by two foot-long, brick-red shaft of cured pork was stretched out on a wooden table like a, er, telephone pole. Customers were all crowding around it while a grocery store associate wearing a blue and white-striped apron and a little white paper hat delicately shaved off thin slices and handed them out.

It was massive. I had never seen anything like it before. Clearly neither had Lulu. She pointed to it and yelled at me, "Mama! Look! A giant meat rocket!"

That was it. Lulu's innocent, yet illicit, innuendo, combined with Rick James' freaky song blaring over the store's speakers, was just too much for me.

"She's a Super Freak, Super Freak,
She's super freaky. Yowww!"

Lulu wanted us to get a sample, but I had turned into a junior high school student. I was laughing so hard at the improbable combination of sights and sounds that I couldn't bring myself to wait in line for a taste of the meat rocket, er, telephone pole, er—straighten up, Gina!—*salami*.

◆ ◆ ◆ ◆ ◆ ◆ ◆ ◆ ◆

"I'm hungry! Please give me something UNHEALTHY."

◆ ◆ ◆ ◆ ◆ ◆ ◆ ◆ ◆

EIGHTEEN

POSSESSIONS DIMINISHED
BY POSSESSION

٭   ٭   ٭   ٭   ٭   ٭   ٭   ٭   ٭   ٭   ٭   ٭

GRAMMA SHEILA GAVE ME LIGHT UP SHOES
AND YOU DID NOT

S UDDENLY THEY WERE EVERYWHERE. They were
lining the grocery store check-out counters, stuffed in vending machines along our main pedestrian drag, the Corso Italia,
and stacked high in tight rows inside the *Tabaccherie* (the tobacco-
nists' shops, which sell all sorts of things beyond cigarettes).

How is it that a mountain range of cheap plastic jewelry,
brightly colored Slinkies, and tiny stamp pads of kittens and pup-
pies had burst its way onto the scene, seemingly overnight? I had
never noticed them before, and I might still not be noticing them,
if not for the plaintive cries below me at about thigh-level from a
certain four-year-old girl.

"Oh, I wish I wish I could have a Slinky, Mama," Lulu

lamented to me one morning. "Allegra has a rainbow one."

Ah, Allegra. Lulu's best friend who is also a source of constant comparison and then desire. It started with, "Allegra has light up shoes," one day.

"Allegra has light up shoes," Lulu repeated. "Pleeeeeze, can I also have light up shoes?"

This went on for about a week with Scotty and me searching around the handful of childrens' shoe stores in Arezzo. We couldn't find any that were in Lulu's size and reasonably priced. I finally called my mom, and she mailed off a brightly colored pair of Skechers from JC Penney.

"You know what?" Lulu said, as she opened the package when it arrived. "Gramma Sheila gave me light up shoes and you did not. She loves me the most."

She wore them proudly for about three days and then suddenly decided they were "too loose" (they were about half a size too big) and refused to wear them. Scotty and I put them back in her closet and planned to have her try them again in a few months.

"Allegra has a *Trilli* (Tinkerbell's name here in Italy) backpack," came next. We were fortunately able to duck that one by reminding Lulu she already had a lovely Winnie the Pooh backpack, and that if she was a good girl, perhaps we'd get her a new one for the next school year. Whew.

And now: "Allegra has a rainbow Slinky." Among the three latest Allegra-driven requests, the Slinky seemed like an easy one to fulfill.

Later that afternoon, Lulu and I got into the car with Allegra and her mother, Michela, to go to swim lessons. A little, plastic, star-shaped Slinky was lying on the floor in the back under Allegra's car seat.

"See, Mama!" Lulu exclaimed as if she'd just discovered the Holy Grail. "There one is! Go to the store and ask for one. And it's not called a Slinky here. It's called a *Mola*."

Good to know.

I got into the front seat and asked Allegra's mother where she bought it. "Oh, you can find them everywhere," she told me. "And they only cost about a Euro."

Perfect. That settled it. A Slinky it was. The next morning, after I dropped Lulu off at school, I headed out to the *centro storico,* or historic center of town, which is lined with shops. Most of the places sell Italian fashions, shoes, antiques, or Tuscan specialties like *pecorino* cheese and *salumi,* but I knew where the one toy store (called Bindi) is, so I made that my first stop.

Oscar, the owner, called out a warm *"Buongiorno"* as I walked in. He knows me. I'm a regular. Not because I'm always in there shopping for Lulu, but because Lulu gets invited to a different classmate's birthday party, or *festa de compleanno*, practically every week and I'm always in there shopping for somebody else.

"I'm looking for a little present today for Lulu, actually," I told him. "Do you have a toy called a Slinky?" I couldn't remember the Italian word Lulu told me to call it, but, apparently, seeing me make the goofy gesture of trying to balance each end of a Slinky in my outstretched hands did the trick.

Oscar led me to the back of the store where there were several of them in a bright little box. No rainbow-patterned ones, however, so I selected a lavender one with orange flowers (since when did these things become so colorful, I wondered). I paid my money and asked Oscar to wrap it.

I hid it under Lulu's pillow and told her that night that it was a special present Daddy magically had delivered as he was out of town that day. She ripped open the paper and happily chirped, "A Slinky! Oh, thank you! And I like the pretty flowers!"

Mission accomplished, I thought.

But, from her room early the next morning, I heard one word: "Tangled."

Then, "Taaaang-led!"

And finally, "TAAAANGLED!"

Lulu came marching out her door, toward me, holding out the Slinky which had somehow managed to become a jumbled curlicue knot.

"Fix it, Mama," she demanded. "Fix it 'cause I wanna take it to school to show Allegra and everyone."

"Fix it, *please*," I corrected.

"Fix it, *please,*" Lulu replied. "*Now.*"

This was no easy task. I examined the jumble and determined it had to be completely rewound from end to end: re-orienting, twisting, and tugging each plastic coil along the way. I started to not like the Slinky.

I handed it back to Lulu.

"Oh," she said looking down at it. "It still not right. Here ya go." She tried to hand it back to me.

"Lulu, honey, it's just the tippy top that's a little tucked under. You can fix that," I said.

"No, you do it. *Please.*"

I reluctantly took it back and un-tucked the top little coil, which had just slightly dipped under the coil beneath it. A small thing, really, but I've become annoyed. "Okay, now, be careful. Don't get it tangled again," I said.

When I arrived to pick Lulu up after school, I see her Winnie the Pooh (not Tinkerbell*)* backpack hanging on the hook outside her classroom. The Slinky had been shoved into an outside pocket and was again in a state of jumbledness. "Oh man," I thought, "I might as well just do this now." I stood there in the hallway and painstakingly unraveled the thing as other parents walked past me with looks ranging from compassion to confusion.

I pleaded with Lulu as I handed it back to her while we walked down the steps from school. "Please, please be careful with it."

"That's okay, Mama," Lulu said. "You can put it back in my *zainetto* (backpack). I want a *Nikula* now."

"What's a *Nikula*?" I hesitantly asked.

"It's a bracelet that's all curly," Lulu said. "Emma has two of them."

Oh, Lord, the Slinky was already obsolete. And now it's not just Allegra who is the trend-setter; little Emma is also involved in this conspiracy. I didn't even know what this latest "must-have" thing was. At least with shoes and backpacks I had a clue. We headed up the hill toward Parco il Prato while Lulu continued gnashing her teeth about these *Nikula*s, or whatever they were.

In front of the snack bar at the park stood a row of toy vending machines. I swear they weren't there the last time we were at the park. But this day, not only were they there, but, as Lulu excitedly pointed out, one happened to be full of those mysterious bracelets. I looked down at the price sticker on the machine, and it reads that for just one small Euro coin, a pair of them can be mine. I mean, Lulu's.

"Please! Mama, oh Please! Look how cute!"

I don't agree. They just look like pastel-colored, repurposed old telephone cords. Which is funny, of course, because Lulu doesn't even know what a telephone cord is.

When we lived in Baltimore, Scotty was driving us home from the book store one afternoon, when we passed an old phone booth. The little silver metal and glass closet was standing dejectedly next to a bus stop, clearly long-abandoned with spray paint now decorating its exterior.

"What's that?" Lulu asked.

"It's a place where you used to go to use the phone," I explained.

"Like when it rains," Lulu said, not understanding that people didn't duck in there with their mobiles in a downpour. Back in the day, a big black phone would be in a booth, hanging on the wall, waiting for you to pick up the receiver connected by a curly cord and put some money in the coin slot on top. This was in the year 1980 B.C., "Before Cell" phones.

"Yes, that's right," I simply replied, just to be done with it.

And now here I was about to buy a couple of old telephone cords for Lulu to wear around her wrists.

That evening, I was sipping a glass of wine at my friend Pavlina's house. Her son, David, who goes to the same preschool as Allegra, Emma, and Lulu, was playing Thomas the Tank Engine with Lulu in the other room. I mentioned the bracelets to Pavlina and she laughed out loud.

"Oh, all the kids have them now. David just got several of them yesterday," she said. "His *nonno* (grandfather) bought them for him when they were out shopping together."

By the time we were about to leave Pavlina's, Lulu and David had traded each other for bracelets in colors they liked better, and David had given an extra one to Lulu. So now they each had three.

I was convinced that this whole crazy kiddie-consumerism-conspiracy was not perpetrated by the children; it's perpetuated by us weak adults. We, who should spend time reasoning and explaining with our kids about the notion of quality and value or saving for something special, instead, just pull out a Euro (or a dollar back in the States) and plunk it over for the next junky plastic item that little Billy, little Suzy, or in my case, little Lulu, is whining for. To keep them quiet until they need their next fix.

I am among the most guilty, I know. I've bought cheapy pink and blue stamp pads from Sandro who runs the *Tabaccheria* near our house. Lulu stamped out a kitten and a Chihuahua for a couple of days and then threw the pads into the blue storage bin under her bed. I've bought Zoobles, colorful small spheres that, when pushed, burst into some kind of unique character. Lulu rolled them around and cooed at them for about a week, then, plop, into the blue bin they went. And on and on.

I had opened Pandora's Box, and it was full of plastic crap.

It was coming to the breaking point in my mind a week or so after Lulu's playdate with David, as we were leaving our house one morning for school, when Lulu started in with a new entreaty.

"Mama, can we go get me a slap-bracelet after school?"

By this time, both the Slinky and those phone cord bracelets had been abandoned, like that phone booth, into the blue storage bin under the bed. I was fed-up with the constant stream of requests.

"A slap-bracelet!?!" I sputtered. "You already have those other bracelets, those *Nikula* ones, or whatever they're called, and you never wear them."

"I will if I have the slap-bracelets too. I need more different kinds," Lulu helpfully explained. "A pink slap-bracelet that is *brillante* (sparkly) is what I need now."

"But why, Lulu?" I asked. "You already have those three other bracelets and you only have two arms."

"Because Angelica has many," Lulu replied. As if that was all the answer I needed. I didn't even know who Angelica was.

I thought of the philosopher Nietzsche, who wrote about materialism and greed. "Possessions are usually diminished by possession," he wrote. I agreed with the idea that collecting a lot of belongings is not the key to happiness. That, and I was desperate to put an end to Lulu's constant clamoring.

"Lulu," I began in my tone that signaled I was about to give a thoughtful dissertation about the ways of the world, specially designed to help her become a better person, "it's not good to always want more *toys*. There are other things in life that will make you happy and there will always be some girl who has more things than you, and you need to get used to—"

Lulu cut me off and interrupted, "Yes! I want to be *that* girl!"

♦ ♦ ♦ ♦ ♦ ♦ ♦ ♦ ♦

*"You know, there are no polka dot houses.
When I am a grown-up, I am going to paint
my house all different colored polka dots."*

♦ ♦ ♦ ♦ ♦ ♦ ♦ ♦ ♦

NINETEEN

MARK TWAIN SAID IT BEST
• • • • • • • • • • • • •
LET US SWEAR WHILE WE MAY, FOR IN HEAVEN IT WILL NOT BE ALLOWED

THE WORD WAS "DAMMIT." Lulu had just dropped her pink plastic watering can that she was filling up at her "tiny sink," also known as the bathroom's bidet, and water had sloshed all over the floor.

"Dammit!" she said again.

"Lulu," I called over my shoulder in the living room, "please don't say that word."

I immediately traveled back in time in my mind to the Lion's Club Field in Farmland, Indiana. It was summer. I had just finished sixth grade. It was at softball practice. And for me, back then, the word was "damn."

I was the second girl to arrive that morning. One of the

self-appointed leaders of the team, a much tougher and much bigger girl than I (who I think might've been a whole year older), named Kelley, was standing on a wooden bench in one of the dugouts, so I trotted down over there to join her. Every other little girl who arrived after me did the same.

We were all scuffing around in the dugout waiting for the coach to appear, when suddenly Kelley placed her hands on her hips and barked, "Why is everyone in this *damn* dugout?!" It was as if she was asserting that *she* was the reason we had chosen to congregate there.

I heard a voice loudly retort, "Well, don't think it's just because of you, Kelley. We all just happen to *want* to be in this *damn* dugout. That's why!"

In horror, I instantly felt my heart start to pound and my teeth clench up with the realization that *I* had said those words. Not only had I just talked back to big tough Kelley, but I also used the "damn" for the first time. Out loud. In front of witnesses.

Kelley seemed not to care that I had smarted off to her. She leaned down at me, smiled with an almost incredulous look of care and real surprise, and said, "Well, little Gina London, I didn't know you cussed."

"Well, I don't. Not really."

"But you just did, didn't you?"

"Yeah, I guess so, but it was only *damn*, right?"

"Oh, *damn* counts, and I am so going to tell your mom."

My mom spent her summers volunteering with other moms to sell Cokes and candy at the Lion's Club concession stand during softball games. We all bought our Marathon bars and Bubs Daddy sticks of grape or watermelon-flavored gum from my mom to chew while we hung out doing nothing in the outfield. Everybody in Farmland knew my mom, but, then again, in a town of 1,200 people, everybody knew everybody.

Andrea, Brad, and I had been raised pretty conservatively by Mom and Dad. We went to the Methodist church on Sundays and to Vacation Bible School in the summers. As far as I knew, that's how everyone was. It was certainly how it seemed in Farmland. After Dad died, only about six months before my great public cussing incident, Mom began leaning even more heavily on the church for support. In addition to Sunday mornings, now we started going to church services in the evenings on Sunday and to prayer meetings on Thursday nights, too. We weren't "preacher's kids," but we had definitely become "churchy" kids, and I, as the eldest, had a clean-cut reputation to maintain. So, I suppose I shocked my young softball cohort when I dared to say "damn." I certainly shocked myself.

By the time I reached the frenzied network newsrooms of CNN

in Atlanta, however, cursing for me had become an art form.

In any line of work, there's most likely a range of employees. Some are soft-spoken, while others are real outspoken loudmouths. From my perspective, journalism seemed to produce some characters especially full of serious salt. Charley Reese, the first syndicated columnist I ever met when I worked at *The Orlando Sentinel,* for instance, was a chain-smoking, crusty old man who desperately clung to his typewriter even as the *Sentinel* brass replaced them with computers. My first television newsroom at WTTG Fox 5 in Washington, D.C., had a captivating crew sprinkled with colorful cynical reporters, hard-drinking video engineers, and aggravated assignment desk editors. I loved them all and I learned a lot, including some interesting ways to express oneself—especially during the hectic clamor of breaking news.

It was a dual existence: how to behave on-air and off-air. A balance that needed to be tightly controlled. Once I reached network news, I learned about the potential pitfall of being *off-air,* but *on-satellite*. It never happened to me, thank goodness, but a CNN reporter colleague got in loads of trouble when he ranted about something in between his live shots. His mic was still hot, and even though the camera wasn't on, his string of epithet pearls was heard, not only by the control room, but by thousands of unsuspecting regular people who had satellite TV and knew how to link up to the "shots in between the shots."

My husband, too, having lived in the variety entertainment world, knew a thing or two (or twelve) about four-letter words. Neither of us are sailors, but an occasional obscenity has been known to be hurled.

After Lulu was born, it didn't seem to matter—at first. She was just a baby meatloaf who couldn't lift herself up, let alone repeat anything articulately. When she was a year old, while we were living in Paris, I didn't think twice about muttering a *damn* if I missed the Metro, or even a more high-caliber *shit* when I blew a fuse in our apartment by daring to have two stove burners going at once.

But when Lulu turned two, that fateful winter afternoon came when it did matter. Light snowfall had blanketed Paris. Lulu and I had just come back home from Square Lambert where we had constructed her first tiny *bonhomme de neige* (snowman) in the park. I unbundled both of us and then prepared some cozy *chocolats chauds* (hot chocolates) to warm us up.

Never a good multi-tasker, I should not have chosen that moment to turn on the computer, but I did. And when I promptly killed our laptop by accidently pouring my mug of hot chocolate in my hand all over the keyboard, I was more angry than surprised. I should've known better. I shouldn't have had that glass anywhere near the computer. Suddenly, just like on that old Indiana softball field, I heard myself cursing. Only this time it was the mother of them all: the F-bomb.

My loud exclamation caught Lulu's attention. She began skipping around the living room, cheerfully repeating the offensive word over and over. I was horrified. I tried massaging my mistake. "No, honey, *Fox*. *Fooox*. Mommy said the word, 'FOX!' The cute, little, red bushy-tailed animal. You know, FOX. FOOOX!"

Her memory was blessedly short, and since then we've both kept that word safely back under lock and key. Well, she has for sure. I have mostly. By three, however, Lulu had developed even more retention and pronunciation abilities. I have tried to discipline myself to change the curse word that's come into my mind into something still explosive, perhaps, but not offensive.

Since we were in Tuscany at this point, I searched for an Italian substitute. *Accidenti* is a great all-purpose word. It's like "damn," although it's perfectly polite, so maybe it's more like "darn." It's used for both negative and positive expressions like, "*Accidenti*, that's a nice car!" or, "*Accidenti*, I just dropped Gramma's vase!" But I couldn't seem to manage to remember to insert it. It just didn't trip off my tongue in a time of crisis like an old, well-loved, and oft-used English word. So, still trying to fend off cuss-words, I tried to deploy "rats!" instead. I figured it has a sharp single-syllable like "damn," and the humor of the word might help me get over whatever grouchy situation has made me explode in the first place.

Yet, in spite of my efforts, the occasional "damn" or "dammit" escaped my lips. I must admit that these expletives must've escaped more than "on occasion," because after the pink water can incident, the next afternoon Lulu sang out again. This time she was trying to wrap a cloth placemat around her bear Vincent's bottom like a diaper. She evidently was having trouble folding it into proper shape, because I could see she was getting agitated. And then, out rang the very distinct, very clear word again from her little pink mouth.

"Dammit!"

"Lulu, honey, don't say that word."

She didn't respond and continued to play silently.

I wondered how much it mattered. She was then only three and trying out new words in English, which for her was probably an unemotional experiment, similar to trying out new vocabulary words at her Italian preschool. I recalled a college drama class during which we had to holler out, in unison, a series of profanities (that I am too shy to type now here in print) with the reasoning that, as the instructor explained, "In acting, words are just so many sounds in a script."

But, then again, this is real life, and even though strong words in Italian, or any other foreign language, don't affect my ear in a particularly harsh way, English words do, especially when spoken by a child.

As adults, we're able to gauge our audience and choose suitable words. Little kids don't deploy such discretion. So, I concluded that I would not simply look the other way; I would try to set a better example and provide loving parental guidance if Lulu said a "bad word" again. And, of course, she did.

This time, she was sitting on the tile floor trying to fit the pieces of her jumbo Disney Babies puzzle together, which our neighbor Martina got Lulu for her birthday. She was trying to squeeze Baby Goofy's head onto Baby Donald's body and of course it wasn't working.

"Daaa-miiit!" my little darling screamed out.

"Lulu, don't say dammit. It's a naughty word."

"But why? I think 'dammit' is such a cutie word," Lulu countered. "It sounds like a little sheep. 'Daaaaaahhhhh-mit!'" And then she 'baaaed' like a perfectly adorable, wooly orator.

As a preschooler, she seems more in touch than I am with that college drama professor. Words, to Lulu, are just sounds with which to create, much like a poet. I silently agreed that "dammit" does have a smooth sound in the middle: "aaaaaahhh." But, I am going to continue working with her, and on myself, with using it sparingly.

But I must say, I think Lulu's response was such a great one that I only wish I could go back in time and tell it to Kelley in that damn softball dugout in Indiana.

129

◆ ◆ ◆ ◆ ◆ ◆ ◆ ◆ ◆

(While angry at me)

"You know who is not shiny? You are not shiny. I am shiny because I am lovely and I know all the kitty songs."

◆ ◆ ◆ ◆ ◆ ◆ ◆ ◆ ◆

TWENTY

A CHRISTMAS WITCH FOR YOU
❖ ❖ ❖ ❖ ❖ ❖ ❖ ❖ ❖ ❖ ❖ ❖
SANTA CLAUS ISN'T THE ONLY ONE COMIN' TO TOWN

IN THE UNITED STATES, of course, he's known as Santa Claus. When we lived in France, Lulu called him *Père Noël*, and now here in Italy, he is adorably known as *Babbo Natale*. I say "adorably" because the word "babbo" is a very special Tuscan contribution that doesn't translate simply as "father." It has a more endearing and intimate meaning, like "daddy." Therefore, the Italian holiday gift-giver isn't "*Father* Christmas," he's "*Daddy* Christmas."

He's also "extremely chubby" as Lulu said one December day. And it was true. As Arezzo shopkeepers started putting up their holiday decorations around the Corso Italia and other roads within the town's medieval historic center, all the red-costumed, white-bearded Babbos' protruded, paunchy tummies were just like the image of our American, jolly old elf made famous by Clement Moore, Thomas Nast, and the Coca-Cola company. We were standing outside of the Rustica Bottega Toscana watching a large, animated Santa Claus, er, *Babbo Natale*, play the saxophone.

"He must eat a lot of pasta," Lulu observed. "And gelato." I had been working on Lulu to try to get her to eat more "healthy foods," and I admit I had mentioned that a daily diet of ice cream or spaghetti with butter and parmesan would not help her grow fit and strong, but could make her become soft and "chubby." I didn't want to give her a complex, but I did want to stress "you are what you eat." With her observation about the apparent poor eating habits of this robotic Santa, it appeared she'd received the message.

"Mama, is it true," Lulu began, "that if you are too chubby, your heart will get squeezed and you will get dead?"

Okay, I also admit that I may have talked about cholesterol clogged-arteries and how excess body fat can lead to heart attacks, but I promise I wasn't trying to scare my four-year-old into eating vegetables. Well, maybe a little. And now here she was worried about old Saint Nick.

"Well, yes, Lulu," I replied, not sure where I was going to go with this. I mean, I had never said that being overweight made someone a bad person, just that it was unhealthy. But, how do I balance the conflicting concepts that an obese old man—who obviously has not been making good eating choices—was still wise and wonderful enough to deliver toys to all the good little girls and boys of the world?

"It's true that it can be dangerous for your heart if you are too chubby, and so I think Santa, er, *Babbo Natale*, is probably on a diet."

"That's good, Mama," Lulu looked visibly relieved. "I don't want *Babbo Natale* to die."

I knew it. She was afraid the old man might keel over before he could fly around the world and bring her her loot.

"He's not going to die, Lulu," I said. "Santa Claus, er, sheesh, *Babbo Natale,* whatever his name is, is going to live for a long, long time. I don't think he'll ever die."

"He will if he keeps eating everything bad for his body," Lulu said.

That night Scotty helped Lulu write *Babbo Natale* a letter. Lulu dictated and Scotty wrote. First, she requested that *Babbo* bring her a snake, and then she asked, "Are you eating anything healthy to help you get skinny?"

Fortunately, later that month, when *Babbo Natale* visited Lulu and her classmates at Bianca Maria Bianchini preschool, he gave each little child a wooden toothbrush and toothpaste holder with a tiny egg-timer fastened to the front. It was designed to help the child brush longer, so for me, that was a clear sign of promoting good health. I mentioned it to Lulu.

"See, *Babbo Natale* wants you to have clean teeth. That's a healthy thing!"

"He was still chubby," Lulu said.

We looked forward to another personal *Babbo Natale* sighting that week as Scotty, Lulu, and I made our way to Arezzo's public library. The *sezione ragazzi*, or children's section, had been advertising that *Babbo* was going to make an appearance that evening and read a story to the kids. The library is in a 500-year-old, former government palace festooned with carved coats of arms from the past centuries of ruling families on its stone exterior. It is a magnificent building, and while I doubted they would feature a sleek and svelte Santa, I imagined a visit that would be especially traditional and memorable.

Well, it was definitely memorable. From the moment *Babbo Natale* stepped through the door, it was plainly obvious to both Scotty and me that this petite person wearing a baggy red suit and white beard was no *babbo,* but was instead a *mamma.* We raised our eyebrows and stifled laughs. The kids were already seated in a semi-circle around a large empty chair that "*Babbo*" proceeded to daintily perch upon. He/she asked the children what they wanted for *Natale*, read them a story in a high-pitched voice, and then passed out *caramelle* (candies). I hoped maybe Lulu hadn't noticed.

"Looks like *Babbo Natale* has lost some weight (and height)," I said to her afterward, holding her in my arms.

Lulu leaned into my ear and whispered, "He was a *girl*, Mama." She had noticed.

Finally, the morning of Lulu's first Italian Christmas arrived and she awoke to discover that the real, chubby, male *Babbo Natale* had somehow managed to survive another season—at least long enough to deliver Lulu her loot. *Babbo* left her the pink scooter she had been clamoring for, after she thankfully tired of the snake idea. Lulu also got a pink children's digital camera with more bells and whistles than our grown-up one, thanks to my mom and my stepdad, Jerry. Scotty's parents, my sister, and our cousins rounded out the rest of her presents in assorted books and toys. It was a real holiday haul.

But it wasn't over. *Babbo Natale* is a relative new-comer to Italy's wintertime gift-giving tradition. Long before they adapted and renamed our American Santa Claus, Italians had *La Befana* to deliver sweets and presents to children in their stockings.

La Befana is an old woman who rides around on a broomstick and leaves goodies for the kiddies on the eve of Epiphany in January. But, in spite of what you might think, our Italian friends point out that she is not a witch. She just needs the broom to fly on and then apparently uses it to sweep the floors of everyone's home before she leaves. She is always depicted smiling and wearing a patched, soot-speckled dress, because she comes down so many chimneys. Instead of leaving cookies and milk for her like Santa Claus, Italians set out a glass of red wine. So, while she may not be a witch, she is tidy and likes a little *vino*: definitely my kind of woman.

Oh, and she is also usually portrayed as thin. I mean, she only has a broomstick to ride, not a giant sleigh pulled by reindeer, so it makes sense. I hadn't made any big deal about that particular distinction when right around this time, Lulu and I met *La Befana* in person. We were at the *Magnifico* shopping center when a woman wearing wire-rimmed spectacles and dressed in a black shawl and peasant-type dress came by to give Lulu a treat. She appeared not to be some random, shabbily-clothed stranger, but to have been sponsored by the shopping center. Trailed by kids, she was holding a broom in one hand and a large canvas sack of treats in the other. She was also beautiful, lithe, and athletically zipping around on roller skates.

Lulu, who was only just learning about *La Befana*, looked up at her in awe. The not-quite-a-witch was lovely, lean, and kind. A holiday heavyweight she could happily believe in. The woman smiled down at Lulu and patted her head. She said something in Italian that I didn't catch and reached into her bag.

She gave Lulu an orange.

Lulu looked back up at *La Befana* and quietly said, "*Grazie.*" Then she looked over at me and said in English, "I like Santa Claus better."

Chubbiness and all.

♦ ♦ ♦ ♦ ♦ ♦ ♦ ♦ ♦

(To Daddy on the phone)

"Are you far away or close away?"

♦ ♦ ♦ ♦ ♦ ♦ ♦ ♦ ♦

TWENTY-ONE

LA GIOSTRA DEL SARACINO
• • • • • • • • • • •
WHAT'S A SARACINO?

L ULU AND I WERE STROLLING and strollering toward the little plaza, Piazzetta San Michele, along the Arezzo's elegant pedestrian street, Corso Italia, when we were suddenly confronted by a large, boisterous procession of men.

"Look, Mama!" Lulu pointed as her mouth dropped open. "A parade!"

There were no floats or high school marching bands, but indeed, walking in precise formation up the hill toward us, were rows and rows of brightly outfitted men. Some were waving and throwing dazzlingly decorated flags, others were beating a rhythm on drums hanging from their necks, while still others were blowing a fanfare on stretched-out, medieval-looking trumpets. All were wearing vibrant tights, short black boots, and long colorful tunics that flared out at the end.

It was like we had just walked into one of those Renaissance Festivals in the States. We would now have to find a place to park in some field, pay for tickets, place dried-flower crowns with ribbons hanging down upon our heads, throw a double-sided ax at a bale of straw, and of course, gnaw on a giant turkey leg.

But no, this was for free, for real, and seemingly completely random. Well, we are in Italy, for heaven's sakes, so maybe it wasn't random at all. Maybe this kind of thing happens here all the time. I later learned that it doesn't happen all the time, but it wasn't random either. Our wonderful friend Francesca, from Arezzo's Tourist Welcome Center, informed us that this parade proclaimed the start of festivities for the city's bi-annual medieval joust tournament, *La Giostra del Saracino,* or Joust of the Saracen.

It was all very interesting and prompted a series of questions from you-know-who.

"So exactly absolutely what is a *Giostra?"* Lulu asked after Francesca told us about it.

"Well, in English, we call them 'jousts,'" I replied. "It's when a knight gallops out on a horse carrying a really long stick called a lance and aims it at another rider who is also holding a lance and riding a horse toward the first guy."

"So they're pointing pointy sticks at each other?" Lulu summed up. Her eyes narrowed. "If they get poked, that will hurt, right?"

"Well, yes, I suppose it would, Lulu, uhm, yes," I said.

"They could get dead even, couldn't they?" she continued.

"Well, uhm, I suppose so, Lulu, yes, maybe they could," I said, knowing that I needed to find a way to switch focus. "But that was a kind of a joust from a long time ago. Arezzo's joust is not that dangerous now, right, Francesca?" I looked over to Francesca with that pleading sort of "help me out" face.

"Oh, no, our men aim their lances toward a *Saracino* statue now, not a real-live person," Francesca said.

"Oh. Okay," Lulu said. Then she added, "What's a *Saracino?"*

"Well, it's a...a...I don't really know actually, Lulu," I confessed.

"In English, it means a 'Saracen'," Francesca offered.

Oh, well, that clears it right up, I thought. Huh?

"What's a *Saracen?"* Lulu asked next—naturally.

Francesca handed us a flier written in English to help explain the event. We took it home to read through it. It was of no help.

In fact, it was written in that kind of "English" you find in so many unfortunate brochures and tour guides that have been written by non-native English speakers. The kind that leaves you asking more questions about the subject than you had before you starting reading it. This one, while practically incomprehensible, also made me laugh. For instance, it referred to the men who rode with the lances as "joustrators," not knights, being knocked from their horse was described as "unhorsement," and then there still remained that mystery surrounding the title of the "joustrators'" opponent. Who in the world is a "Saracen" and why are Arezzo's knights jousting toward him?

I'm sure there are medieval scholars out there who already know the answer, but I had to Google the word to find out. "Saracen" was the word used to describe the enemy of the Crusades. And if you don't remember your history from that time, which I admit I didn't, just who exactly did the Christian Crusaders consider their enemies? According to the same source, the "Saracens" were simply Arabs or Muslims.

Ouch. So this tournament centers on trying to attack an Arab? Yikes. Having lived and worked in the Middle East, where I met scores of wonderful people—all of whom happened to be Arab and many of whom also happened to be Muslim—I was more than a little taken aback.

"So, Mama," Lulu said again, when she noticed I had looked up from my research at home. "What is a 'Saracen?'"

There was no way I could think to delicately describe the biases during the Crusades compared with now, especially since many of those same sentiments have unfortunately endured. I oversimplified:

"Oh, it's just a 'bad-guy.'"

Lulu seemed satisfied, but I wasn't. Every English-speaking tourist who reads that brochure is going to have no idea what the joust is about. I did some more online research about the event and, in spite of the xenophobia issue, I grew more and more convinced that Arezzo's Joust of the Saracen Tournament was a tremendous spectacle of pageantry and skill—and deserved to be described and promoted better in its English translations. Everyone seems to have heard about the medieval event in Siena, so why not here?

I marched back into the city's Tourist Welcome Center and announced to Francesca that I would happily rewrite their English flier, free of charge, just for the opportunity to help out and learn more about the *Giostra*. She became excited. She said she had always disliked the way that version read, and, in turn, marched me over to the city's Department of Tourism, where she introduced me to its director, Alessandro.

Alessandro appeared excited too when Francesca got to the part about me redoing the flier *for free*. He said not only would he be delighted to have me rewrite the brochure, but would I also possibly be interested in rewriting the English version of *the city's entire new website*?

Before I had taken a moment to fully consider that undertaking, I felt my head nodding in the affirmative.

So, I whipped out a new crisp, clean, and more conversational version of the joust brochure. I tidied up its clunky translations. "Joustrators" became "knights," and the while the word "dehorsement" became a little longer, I thought the phrase "when a rider falls off his horse" was a bit clearer.

I also tried to shift focus from its biased battle origins to the beauty of the event itself: "Welcome to Arezzo's Famous Joust of the Saracen. Pageantry of the Middle Ages for Modern Times," I wrote. I then gave a brief history of the bi-annual joust with a brief explanation of why the giant mannequin aimed at by the knights is referred to as a *Saracino*, or Saracen. I wrote, "The event was born in the Middle Ages when knights of the Crusades dashed off to vanquish the 'Infidels' or 'Saracens.' Of course, now our tournament…is for fun and sport." I hoped that would move the reader along and not cause him to pause and ponder the Saracen's particular ethnicity or religion.

It only took me a couple of days to rewrite the brochure and along the way I told Lulu about the things I learned.

"During the week of the joust, there will be a lot of parades," I said.

"Good, I like parades. A lot," Lulu said.

"And on the day of the joust, cannons will sound off each activity," I said.

"Real cannons? Like on pirate ships?" Lulu asked. "I like pirates a lot, too. They're like knights, but on boats."

"Uhm, okay," I said.

So, the flier was a joy. Rewriting the website, however, was not. In fact, it became something of a Herculean task.

Obviously, I wasn't mucking out dung from the stables of immortal cows, but, after a month, I began to feel as overwhelmed. As soon as I finished one section, the department emailed me a new one. And then another. And another. It did seem a little like Hercules' struggles after all, since the versions I received read like a never-ending pile of immortal cow sh—no, never mind. Let's just say, I had a lot more work to do revising myriad topics than I had revamping a single jousting tournament.

I wrote about Arezzo's history: the ancient Etruscans; wars between the *Aretini* locals and the powers from Florence; and the ubiquitous Medici. I wrote about Arezzo's Renaissance: since the city is on the route between Rome and Florence, nearly every Italian master painter, architect, or writer passed through its walls. Michelangelo was born in its valleys, Leonardo da Vinci painted its countryside, and before Dante wrote his *Divine Comedy*, he fought here in the Battle of Campaldino. I wrote about churches, food, wine, and antique fairs. I wrote about restaurants, hotels, and villas. I even wrote about where to find parking and what to do in case of an emergency.

In the meantime, Lulu and I watched more colorful processions with the musicians and flag-throwing *Sbandieratori*. We also made our way up to the bleachers now erected and surrounding *Piazza Grande,* or Arezzo's Grand Plaza. City workers had also created a long dirt track—stretching from one end of the large plaza to the other—transforming it into the jousting arena. We gasped at the *prove,* or knight's jousting practices, in which they rode their horses at full-gallop uphill toward the hulking torso of "Buratto, King of the Indies," also known as our dear friend the Saracen.

Buratto (his official name) is carved in wood and mounted on a post that swivels. He's wound up tight as a top and holds three leather balls hanging from chains, like a flail, in his outstretched right hand. The score shield is in his left. The knight charges toward the shield aiming for the bull's eye. He must jab it really quickly and get out of there before Buratto whips around and wallops the knight with his menacing weapon.

It was a lot more exciting and dangerous than I had imagined.

"Is that true, Mama," Lulu began after witnessing a practice run, which saw the knight make a really close call with Buratto's, er, balls, "that that man could really get hurt from the Saracen?"

"Well, he is riding pretty fast," I said. "So, I think he'll get past before Buratto can whack him."

"But if he got hit, he could get dead, right?" Lulu prodded. Here we go again.

"No, honey, I don't think he would be killed by it. It just might sting a little," I replied, trying to navigate another round of jousting doom and gloom.

At the end of watching two days of *prove,* we saw plenty of action, but thankfully no disasters. Lulu loved it. I did, too.

As for rewriting the website, I thought I would be finished by the end of March. But it took me an extra couple of weeks, until the middle of April.

"You're late, Mama," Lulu scolded me.

"That's okay, Lulu," I said. "Italians understand late. They like late. They're always late."

It's true. One of the first things you'll notice and either embrace or hate about Italy is that everything has a "late" kind of flair. Most stores don't open until around 10:00 a.m., or whenever the owner feels like it. Italians take their lunches late, sometime between 1:00 and 3:00 p.m. They also all close their stores during that time, not reopening until after four in the afternoon. Nearly every train I've taken has been late. When the announcement comes over the intercom, people just look at each other, smile, and shrug their shoulders. Italian events start late—often because people are still arriving thirty minutes after the posted start time—but also often by design, and even for children's programs.

I walked past an enchanting poster one day advertising a theater production of *Il Piccolo Principe* (or *Le Petit Prince* or *The Little Prince,* depending on your preferred version) and was preparing to ask Scotty if we could take Lulu to it, when I noticed the starting time. Nine o'Clock? In the evening? That's when it begins? We later learned that was the norm. So, I figured I would be all right with being a little late delivering my website rewrite. And, yes, I was fine. Although it had originally been planned for the beginning of the month, the new website wasn't officially launched until the end of May.

After months of watching joust practices, rewriting the tournament, and even jumping into the deep-end of the Arezzo cultural immersion pool by writing the tourism department's entire English website, I was beginning to really feel like a part of Arezzo. A part of Italy. Warmly wrapped in the power of its traditions.

Then, just one week before the tournament itself, I received word from Francesca that the city wanted to give me tickets. Me. Tickets. VIP tickets even. To the *Giostra.* I was elated. Now, I really felt that I was a part of this Tuscan community.

The morning of the Joust of the Saracen arrived and Lulu and I rushed off to get up to the cathedral's plaza. At 11:00 a.m., a child was to draw names and the Herald of the Joust was scheduled to officially announce in which order the knights would charge our buddy Buratto. Then each jousting team, with its members dressed in full Renaissance regalia, would formally parade past the gathered spectators. I didn't want to miss it. We were just about to round the bend to begin climbing the short hill to the *duomo*, or cathedral, when the cannon sounded-off, signaling it was 11:00 a.m.

"Oh, no, we're late," I said.

"Yay, we're late! We're Italian!" Lulu spontaneously cried.

And wouldn't you just know that this time they actually started an event on time. Fortunately, we only missed a little. And now by attending Arezzo's famous joust tournament *and* arriving late, we had become as close as we'll ever get to being truly Italian.

◆ ◆ ◆ ◆ ◆ ◆ ◆ ◆ ◆

"I'm four, but I know things."

◆ ◆ ◆ ◆ ◆ ◆ ◆ ◆ ◆

EPILOGUE

THE END OF A
VERY GOOD YEAR

❖   ❖   ❖   ❖   ❖   ❖   ❖   ❖   ❖   ❖   ❖   ❖

I AM SITTING OUTSIDE UNDER a cream-colored canvas umbrella at my favorite Arezzo restaurant, Caffe dei Costanti. While it's only 11:00 a.m., it's also the middle of July and *gia caldo*, or already extremely hot. I'm sipping an icy cold *shakerato* coffee drink that my friend and favorite waiter, Silvio, has brought to me. The café's terrace faces out onto Piazza San Francesco, one of the most popular gathering places in the town's *centro storico*, or historic center. I have waved and called out a friendly "*Ciao!*" and "*Buongiorno!*" to Pietro, the café's owner, who is strolling around the patio. To Gigi, who owns the antique store next door. To my friend Paola, who has ridden by on her bicycle in her customary, fashionable high heels and chandelier earrings.

I take another refreshing sip and look across the other side of the piazza to the Church of San Francesco. Inside is the famous Early Renaissance series of frescoes, "The Legend of the True Cross," by Piero della Francesca. Scores of people are milling about the church's large wooden doors waiting to go in. Some are wearing white cotton hats to protect their heads. Men are in T-shirts, and ladies in skirts or sun-dresses. Most everyone has sensible walking shoes, be they sandals or sneakers. Children are squealing and running about and getting reprimanded with finger snaps to come back. Snippets of many different languages float over my way. Tourists. Here for only a moment or perhaps a day or two. To check off the must-see sights on their lists and travel on.

But we have lived here for a year. And while I am obviously an American and will never be truly considered *una donna Toscana*, or Tuscan woman, I also feel very much at home.

I have been inside *La chiesa di San Francesco* (and all the other churches here in the center of town) dozens of times and throughout the year to view seasonal displays, often with Italian friends as guides. I have spent many hours inside the museums. I have strolled among the furniture, artworks, and oddities to be found in Arezzo's monthly antique fair, which is the oldest and largest in Italy. I have sat in the sun in every *piazza* and smaller *piazzetta*. I have eaten in almost every *trattoria*, *osteria*, and *pizzeria* in town. I have visited every place where a touching scene from the Oscar-winning movie *Life is Beautiful* was filmed. Its director and star, Roberto Begnini, was born in Arezzo province and chose this town—my town now—as the setting for the heart-warming and tragic tale. I attended Arezzo's famous *Giostra del Saracino* tournament with free tickets given to me by the city.

But it has not only been these kind of "when you're abroad," colorful experiences that made this year so enriching. It has been successfully tackling the normal, everyday activities, like we all do, that has made me feel like someone more than a tourist, like a member of the community.

Treks to and from the grocery store, which force me to hike up the steep cobbled streets of the Corso Italia or Via Madonna del Prato, pushing Lulu in her *passeggino* more times than I care to imagine. Standing in line waiting my turn at the *Farmacia* to get something to help combat the treacherous tiger mosquitoes that torture us here. Going to swim lessons. Going to the parks. With Lulu.

Yes. Lulu. This year with and for her has been the most fulfilling part of it all. Watching her go from timid new kid at her preschool to a cheerful, rambunctious rascal has been delightful. She had barely even heard of Italy before we arrived, and now she is fluent in the language, the food, and—after a year of new twists on holiday celebrations—many of the traditions.

She is still from the United States like I am, of course, but in many ways, right now, at this time of her life with her Italian school and

Italian friends, she is more Tuscan than American.

Because it is often your friends who define you. Last April, when Paola had made reservations at a swanky restaurant, "Le Chiave d'Oro," for my birthday dinner, I sat surrounded by new girlfriends. A few were American, one was Canadian, one was Czech, and many were Italian. All were terrific. No matter where in the world I have lived, I have tried to have as authentic an experience as possible. I like to meet people for the sake of meeting kindred spirits from any and everywhere.

And I think Lulu is embracing this outlook as well. She still has friends in Paris where she spent most of the first two years of her life. We still correspond to her playmates from Baltimore, and now, here in Italy, I hope that we're making friends we can keep for a lifetime.

But I'm not going to worry about leaving quite yet. We still have another year ahead for Lulu and me to have plenty more conversations and adventures. Scotty and I will get to watch her grow and develop and say more funny things. She'll get to play for another year with her sweet new friends like Lara, David, Alessio, Max, Letizia, Mathilde, and of course, Allegra.

Lulu knows we have another year left. But she doesn't quite understand what going back to the States will mean.

"Mama, is it true, that in America, they have ice cream?" she asked me recently.

"Yes, honey, they even have gelato."

"When we move back to America, will I still be able to see Allegra and Letizia every day?"

I didn't answer her. But I thought to myself:

No, honey, you will not. But I hope you will always remember that this was a beautiful part of the most wondrous time in your life.

145

Photo by Dan Plehal

GINA LONDON

❖ ❖ ❖ ❖ ❖ ❖ ❖ ❖ ❖ ❖ ❖ ❖ ❖

BECAUSE I'M SMALL NOW AND YOU LOVE ME

Gina London is an Emmy award-winning veteran CNN correspondent and anchor, who is now internationally recognized as a media, presentation, and communications trainer. Among other publications, her work has been featured in *The Denver Post*, *The Orlando Sentinel*, and *In Business Romania*. She lives in Arezzo, Italy, with her husband Scotty Walsh and their indomitable daughter Lulu. Visit her at www.GinaLondon.com. This is her first book.